motivos

THE LIFE OF ST. FRANCIS

Bilingual Press/Editorial Bilingüe

Publisher
Gary Francisco Keller

Executive Editor
Karen S. Van Hooft

Associate Editors
Brian Ellis Cassity
Amy K. Phillips
Linda K. St. George

Address
Bilingual Press
Hispanic Research Center
Arizona State University
PO Box 875303
Tempe, Arizona 85287-5303
(480) 965-3867

motivos

THE LIFE OF ST. FRANCIS

GABRIELA MISTRAL

BILINGUAL EDITION AND ENGLISH TRANSLATION BY ELIZABETH HORAN

Bilingual Press/Editorial Bilingüe

Tempe, Arizona

For original edition information, see p. vii.

Library of Congress Cataloging-in-Publication Data

Mistral, Gabriela, 1889-1957.
[Motivos. English]
Motivos : the life of St. Francis / Gabriela Mistral : Edition and English Translation by Elizabeth Horan.
pages cm
Includes bibliographical references.
Text in English and Spanish.
ISBN 978-1-931010-93-1
1. Francis, of Assisi, Saint, 1182-1226—Poetry. I. Horan, Elizabeth, 1956- translator II. Title.
PQ8097.G6M613 2013
861'.62—dc23

2012040426

Printed in the United States of America

Front cover art: The Key to the Garden *(2010) by Alfredo Arreguín*
Back cover: Gabriela Mistral in Mexico, 1923
Illustration credits appear on p. x.
Cover and interior design by John Wincek

CONTENTS

A NOTE ON THIS EDITION

This volume represents the first time that all forty-four of Gabriela Mistral's *Motivos* have appeared in print in a single text. Some two-thirds were written in Mexico between 1922 and 1924. She composed the latter third from 1926 to 1929, while living between Paris and Provence, where she worked as a foreign correspondent and served in international organizations. The majority were first published shortly after she had composed them. They appeared in various newspapers and periodicals in Mexico, Argentina, and Chile. The poet hoped to finish writing them in Assisi, and to publish the collection as a biography in 1926. She said that she wanted the voice of a Latin American woman to be included in the commemorations of the 700th anniversary of Francis of Assisi's death. Because her other duties intervened, the publication was postponed. As of 1928, she had offered the text as a book to a friend who wanted to publish it, but the project fell through as a result of the political and economic crises surrounding 1929 and her sorrow following her mother's death.

The word *motivos* refers to a "contemplated reality" that sparks a poetic idea and sentimental commentary that are channeled into prose or verse (Barca lxxix). The *motivo* arises from a meditative reverie. The writer's contemplation of the fine details of the natural world provokes a response, the *motivo*, which describes and speculates on the spiritual essence of what is being contemplated. Gabriela Mistral's earliest *motivos* were meditations on dust and mud in the series of prose poems that she called "Motivos del barro," which "turn around the Oriental idea of dust as bringing all things together" and leading toward reincarnation (Arrigoitia 48). Her "Motivos de la Pasión" reconstruct the scene of the meditation in the Garden of Gethsemane and Judas's betrayal of Jesus, animating the story by relating it from the perspective of the olive trees.

Upon Mistral's move to Mexico, she transformed the *motivo* into biographical sketches influenced by immersion in the senses, emulating the compositions of Nervo and inspired by her appreciation of the Mexican countryside. The *Motivos de San Francisco* features almost fifty linked prose poems, poetic meditations on the body, origins, and experiences of the saint, including some scenes from his poems, the "Florecillas." The writer presents those aspects of Francis of Assisi that are closest to theosophy and modernist poetry, showing how love and mercy bring relief from suffering, and how nature, such as the sweet-smelling lilies of the field and the joy of songbirds, is suffused with peace and divine benevolence. Woven into this lyrical contemplation is a mystical, sensual reconstruction of the saint's body. Propelled by feeling and imagination, the *motivos* become a meditative biography, including moments of praise and prayer as well as commentary on the community that Francis developed alongside his close friends.

The Spanish of the present text draws from several previous compilations. From discovering and comparing variant readings and different printings, I found that the most authoritative overall source was usually the earliest published version, noted in bibliographies compiled by Escudero and Arrigoitia and corroborated in the collection of the poet's prose, published in Buenos Aires (Pereira Rodríguez, 1962). Many factors argued for following that edition, which includes lines dropped from later-published versions of the same *motivos*. Also, the only other bilingual collection to include some of Gabriela Mistral's *motivos* follows this first text (Tapscott). Archives now located in the National Library in Chile indicate that Pereira Rodríguez, the editor of this collection, contacted and paid permissions fees to the poet's estate and that the writer Marta Salotti, who had long worked as Mistral's literary representative in Argentina and who knew the writer's habits of composition, was consulted. This early edition also follows standard practice in textual editing, of supplying complete records of original periodical publications. All of these factors suggest that Pereira Rodríguez had access to original texts, and that original periodical publications were consulted.

The first collection to be published as *Motivos de San Francisco* appeared in Santiago three years after the one in Buenos Aires (Díaz-Muñoz Cormatches, 1965). This Chilean edition, a valuable source, is attractively designed and presented. A note in the text suggests that when Doris Dana, the heir and executor to the poet's literary estate, learned of its imminent publication, she declared that Mistral had been working on the *Motivos* at the time of her death. As yet, no such corrected copy has appeared in the writer's files.

Scholars have located further *motivos* published in Mistral's lifetime. Their searches led to the inclusion of another nine *motivos* in the present text. Jaime Quezada includes three *motivos* that had been previously published in *El Mercurio* in the volume *Gabriela Mistral, poesía y prosa*. Like all readers of Gabriela Mistral, I am indebted to him and to the work of Luis Vargas Saavedra, whose close examination of the poet's notebooks and drafts yielded additional episodes from Gabriela Mistral's life of St. Francis, published in *Prosa religiosa de Gabriela Mistral* and *Recados para hoy y mañana*, volume II.

ACKNOWLEDGMENTS

I am grateful to the many friends who have helped in the process of completing this book, which began at an energizing lunch on a beautiful spring day in Tempe, Arizona. During that lunch, organized by my colleagues Claudia Sadowski-Smith and Claire Fox, I met Gary Francisco Keller, who shared his ideas about Franciscanism in the Americas and showed immediate enthusiasm and understanding for the importance of making Gabriela Mistral's *Motivos de San Francisco* available to a wider readership. I thank Jeffrey M. Burns, Director of the Academy of American Franciscan History for quick, clear responses to my questions about the history of Third-Order lay Franciscans. To Taylor Corse, Doris Meyer, Amalia Skilton, and Grace Ditsworth, who each read and offered comments on drafts: thank you many times over. This publication would not be possible without the selfless work of Doris Atkinson, as heir to the estate of Doris Dana, and of Mariano Fernández Amunátegui, Chilean Ambassador to the United States: their efforts have made it possible to obtain the rights to publish Mistral's work in easily accessible formats. Thanks to many hours of careful planning and hard work by Atkinson and Fernández, Gabriela Mistral's legacy will become more broadly and freely available to readers everywhere.

Among far-flung colleagues, I thank Luis Vargas Saavedra for the unpublished paper that he shared with me, and more broadly, for his sharing expertise in our always spirited conversations about Gabriela Mistral. Timely insights from Noël Valis, Santiago Daydí-Tolson, and Martin Taylor reminded me of larger perspectives; thank you. I appreciate the superb hospitality I received from La Casa de Los Amigos in Mexico City, where I stayed while visiting museums and archives, learning more about why and how part of Gabriela Mistral's response to post–Revolutionary Mexico was her conversion or return to Catholicism and her decision to become a Third-Order Franciscan.

At Arizona State University, I am grateful for the warm-hearted administrative support from Neal Lester, Associate Vice President of the Office of Knowledge

Enterprise Development, and Maureen Daly Goggin, English Department Chair, enabling the research that went into this book. The Interlibrary Loan Office at Hayden Library, Arizona State University helped track down sources. I thank Paul Francis Skilton for his daily encouragement. My special thanks go to Cynthia Tompkins for her invaluable expertise and service in checking my translations against the original Spanish. First and last, for Gary Francisco Keller's quickness to understand the importance of Gabriela Mistral in connection with Franciscanism in the Americas and for his steady faith and insights, I am most deeply grateful.

Illustration Credits

p. 2: Reproduced from Francis Jammes, *Le rêve franciscain*, Paris, 1927

pp. 58, 70, 110, and 116: Reproduced from *Lecturas clásicas para niños*, Mexico, 1925

p. 106: Reproduced from *Les Petites Fleurs de Saint François d'Assise*, Paris, 1926

p. 144: Courtesy of Dana/Atkinson Mistral Archives, Biblioteca Nacional de Chile

p. 155: Gabriela Mistral Collection, Department of Special Collections, Charles E. Young Research Library, UCLA

p. 159, top and bottom: Reproduced from the originals held by the Department of Special Collections of the Hesburgh Libraries of the University of Notre Dame

p. 172: Courtesy of Dana/Atkinson Mistral Archives, Biblioteca Nacional de Chile

motivos

THE LIFE OF ST. FRANCIS

Angelina Beloff, *Saint Francis of Assisi*

CAPÍTULO 1

MICHOACÁN, MÉXICO, 1922–1923

THE MOTHER

We must start by praising you, mother of Francis, Italian Maria, as in the Gospel of the other Pobrecillo.

It was you, Madonna Pica, who brought together in your womb that soft lump of flesh who was called Francis of Assisi.

You came down from Provence into the Valley of Umbria. In your youth, its strong winds drummed against you and you walked through the olive groves and the very biblical vineyards of your country. You would carry a pitcher on your shoulder like these women that I watch coming down to the lake. The amphorae grazing their cheeks are like a flower petal's double-crown. The contrast between your grace and his coarseness made the eyes of that coarse man Bernardone light on you.

I praise your breast which has since turned to ashes. Your pure marrow created the outline of Francis's mouth, a mouth delicately fitted for songs. Your milk, as a woman drenched in sunlight, must have been magnificent. You certainly sustained him, so that his youth was rich, intense, like the deepest purple.

We settle, kneeling to kiss his dust, but you, lucky woman, you held him resting on your breast thousands of nights. With your flour you formed in him those fine, white teeth that gave him a happy smile. You established in him the rich blood that became immense charity in his heart. Many aspects of his figure followed yours, and for this reason you can be called "God's Chalice." You taught him to speak, and that hint of sweetness that gathered the birds all around, as if his words were golden hemp and bird seed, came to him from you and not from Bernardone.

And you led him in play. You rounded off the little hill of blond sand that he destroyed and remade. So did you teach him about lines and shapes and make his eye delight in grace. His desire to sing also came from the songs that you surely poured over him when you had him straddling your knees, happy woman, good in giving a son who would sing a joyous tongue to the sad world.

You, Christian woman, glided through the seven gentle years of the childhood of your Christ like a tiny drop of honey entering his ears, which you made as familiar to him as the creases of your neck. And his humility, his intoxication with humility, did it not come from his watching you do your housework, washing floors, sweeping the dining room, as the good wife of a tradesman, who despised none of this?

And I praise your unwavering firmness when the hypocrites, looking to annoy you, came with the alarming news of your Francis's impassioned boyhood.

LA MADRE

Hay que empezar como en el Evangelio del otro Pobrecillo por la alabanza tuya, madre de Francisco, María Italiana.

Fuiste tú, Madona Pica, la que cuajó en sus entrañas este grumo tan suave de carnes que se llamó Francisco de Asís.

Venías de Provenza y bajaste al Valle de la Umbría. En la mocedad te batieron sus robustos vientos y caminaste entre los olivares y las viñas muy bíblicas de tu país. Llevarías un cántaro al hombro como estas mujeres que yo miro bajar al Lago y a las cuales da el ánfora que roza la mejilla la forma de algunas flores de corola bipartida. Por el contraste de su rudeza con tu gracia, se posaron en ti los ojos de aquel rudísimo Pedro Bernardone.

Alabo tu seno hecho cenizas. Su yema pura hizo el contorno de la boca de Francisco, la delicada boca para las canciones. Tu leche de mujer bebedora de soles debió ser magnífica. Lo sustentaste con exceso, y así tuvo él esa rica juventud, intensa como una púrpura.

Nosotros nos conformamos con besar arrodillados su polvo, pero tú, dichosa, le tuviste acostado en tu pecho miles de noches; tú le hiciste con tus harinas esos dientecillos finos y blancos que le daban una sonrisa feliz; tú le pusiste la rica sangre que en su corazón se hizo tremenda caridad; muchas líneas de su cuerpo serían tuyas, y puede llamársete por esto "Copa de Dios". Tú le enseñaste a hablar, y de ti, no del Bernardone, le vino ese dejo de dulzura que le reunía a los pájaros en torno, como si sus palabras fueran alpistes y cañamones dorados.

Y tú le hiciste jugar; redondeabas el montoncito de arena rubia que él desbarataba y volvía a hacer. Así le enseñabas formas y formas y le hacías el ojo amador de la gracia. Su deseo de cantar fue cosa que le vino también de las canciones con las que le anegabas cuando le tenías sobre tus rodillas, mujer dichosa, buena para dar en un hijo cantador una lengua de alegría al mundo triste.

Tú, cristiana, le deslizaste en los siete años dóciles de la infancia a tu Cristo, como una gota de miel imperceptible, por los oídos, y se lo hiciste tan familiar como el pliegue de tu cuello. Y su humildad, su embriaguez de humildades, ¿no le vendría de mirarte hacer tus trabajos de la casa, el lavado de tus pisos, el barrido de tu comedor, buena esposa de mercader, que nada de esto desdeñarías?

Yo te alabo tu falta de arrebatos, cuando te llevaron los hipócritas para irritarte la alarma de la mocedad tan ardiente de tu Francisco. Les oías con calma y sonreías solamente diciendo que con el tiempo se habría de volver un buen hijo del Señor.

You calmly heard them out and you smiled, simply saying that in time he would surely become a good child of the Lord.

And that day came, although it brought you, poor Madonna Pica, yet another trial. Your Francis suddenly let go of everything, all of life's gifts, even your own tenderness. He took to the streets, begging.

Astonished, neighborhood women came to you with the newest scandal without causing any change to your deep sweetness. We thank you for that serving dish with food that you smuggled out from the terrible Bernardone, sending it to your crazy little boy in the cave, and for that subtle cunning which you showed in managing his escape from the merchant's jail.

The valleys have thanked you for those loving hands which you gave him for watering his field. The birds have thanked you for the language with a new song that you put in the wind, and the poor will always thank you for the Healer given over to bandage the wounded world.

Now you're in Heaven at Mary's side and near the mother of St. Julian, patron of hospitality, and you will beam with an eternal smile.

Y vino el día, pero trayéndote, pobre Madona Pica, otra tribulación no más. Porque tu Francisco dejó caer de sus manos, de repente, todos los regalos de la vida, hasta tu misma ternura y se fue por los caminos a pordiosear.

Las comadres, asombradas, te llevaron el nuevo escándalo, sin alterar tu larga dulzura.

Te damos gracias por esa fuentecita de alimentos que a escondidas del terrible Bernardone mandabas a tu loquillo a la cueva, y por aquella tu fina astucia para hacerlo escapar del encierro del mercader.

Te han agradecido los valles esas manos tan amantes que tú diste para regar su campo; los pájaros, la lengua con canción nueva que pusiste en el viento, y los pobres te agradecerán siempre al Vendador, todo él una vendilla para el mundo herido.

Ahora estás en el Cielo al lado de María y cerca de la madre de San Julián, el Hospitalario, y sonreirás con una eterna sonrisa.

Lago Chapala, Michoacán, México, dic. 1922

BODY

What would the body of St. Francis have been like?

They say that it seemed so delicate as to scatter in the wind. It scarcely cast a shadow. Shadows involve pride in things, like the shade of the tree when it paints the lawn or like the woman who, in passing, suddenly blurs the fountain. The Pobrecillo scarcely cast a shadow.

He was small. Like foam crossing water, his presence on the road was more felt than seen in outline.

Arms so light that his sides did not feel their fallen weight; a head nodding gracefully like the tip of the stamen within the flower; legs that skipped without trampling the grass underneath, and his chest was narrow yet broad in showing love (love is an essence, not a water that needs large vessels). And his back . . . it too was narrowed by humility, so that it recalled a small cross, smaller than that Other one.

Ardor burned his flanks to leanness. The flesh of his youth had vanished, together with his youthful sins.

Maybe his small body crackled from the heat, as dry cactus crackles with the heat.

Human happiness is such a weighty thing, and he didn't want it. Pain, another form of density that pulls and tears, was something he fled from. What weighed nothing was this joy in creatures, which he wanted to carry forever.

He would feel the world as light as a crown of flowers. Perched at its edges, he didn't want to weigh more than the sipping bee.

Who sings best in the valleys when the wind passes through? People whose ears are thick say that it's the river, which shatters cups amid its gravel. Others say that it's a woman who thins out a shout in her throat of flesh.

But the one who sings best is the hollow reed, where no depths entangle the voice. The reed that stood in the valley was you, slender Francis, who scarcely scratched the world like the thinnest of shadows.

EL CUERPO

¿Cómo sería el cuerpo de San Francisco?

Dicen que de fino parecía que pudiera dispersarlo el viento. Echaba poca sombra; la sombra es como una soberbia de las cosas, ésa del árbol que pinta el césped o ésa, de mujer que pasa empañando un instante la fuente. Apenas echaba sombra el Pobrecillo.

Era pequeñito. Como cruza un cabrilleo por el agua, cruzaba él por los caminos, y más se le sentía la presencia que se le veía la forma.

Ligeros los brazos tanto que los costados no se los sentían caídos; la cabeza como cabezuela de estambre dentro de la flor, tenía una mecedura llena de gracia; las piernas leves por el pasar siempre sobre las hierbas sin doblarlas, y angosto el pecho aunque fuese tan ancho para el amor (el amor es esencia y no agua que requiera grandes vasos). Y la espalda... también era estrecha por humildad, para que se pensase en una cruz pequeña, menor que la Otra.

Tenía enjutos de arder los costados. La carne de su juventud se había ido junto con los pecados de ella.

Tal vez le crepitaba el cuerpecillo como crepitan de ardor los cactus áridos.

La felicidad humana es una cosa como de gravidez, y no la quiso; el dolor es otra espesura que rinde, y lo huía. Lo ingrávido era ese gozo de las criaturas que quiso llevar siempre.

Solía sentir el mundo ligero como una corola. Y él, posado en sus bordes no quería pesarle más que la abeja libadora.

¿Quién canta mejor en los valles cuando pasa el viento? Los gruesos oídos dicen que es el río que quiebra copas entre sus cascajos; otros dicen que es una mujer que adelgaza el grito en su garganta de carne.

Pero el que canta mejor es el carricillo vaciado, donde no hay entrañas donde la voz se enrede, y ese carricillo que se erguía en el valle eras tú, menudo Francisco, el que apenas rayaste el mundo como una sombrita delgada.

Lago Chapala, Michoacán, México, dic. 1922

TWO LEGENDS

There are two legends about the birth of the boy, which, due to their beauty, deserve to be true.

People will see so strong a parallel with the life of Christ that they will want to make the similarity utterly absolute. The exaggeration that we find in heroic legends speaks of the sublime craving of the humble folk. Educated people work, gnawing away at supernatural deeds. They claim to analyze, simply intending to uncover the truth, but with minds that tend to seem narrow. Their cups are small and they don't want them to overflow. By contrast, the so-called common people weave poems about their betters. Envy isn't known to them, although they're quite dispossessed, and they expand the materials in their adoration. In them, the memory of the divine is less hidden away, so that when they meet something similar, they easily welcome it.

One legend goes like this:

The mother was entering labor and her suffering was lasting longer than was natural. Pica tossed and turned in bed, moaning. One could say that the flesh refused to submit to the one who would surpass it. Then a pilgrim knocked at the door and said that the mother wouldn't give birth until she was taken from her sumptuous bed and brought to the house's stable.

It was done; she was put on the trampled hay among the cows that were mooing, watching the agitation of the birth, and the donkeys that watched the sick woman with their great black eyes.

The other legend is about the child's baptism.

Everything was ready and the shining procession was about to go out when a second pilgrim knocked at the door. More dust and rags than clothes, he said that he wanted to hold the newborn baby's head in the baptismal font.

Pica agreed, and she became obedient to Grace, like the other Mother, and it was the tramp who supported the little body, astonishing the well-to-do people who felt that his presence spoiled the party.

The Church doesn't defend the authenticity of the two stories. The biographers do, only to give a place to those two shining frescoes. They're a good entry into a life whose every episode is made moist by ingenuousness like heavy dew.

DOS LEYENDAS

Hay dos leyendas que por su belleza merecerían ser verdad sobre el nacimiento del niño.

El pueblo verá en su vida paralelismo tal con la de Cristo, que querrá hacer absoluta la semejanza. La exageración que encontramos en las leyendas heroicas, dice el hambre sublime de los humildes. Los letrados trabajan royendo el hecho sobrenatural; aseguran que analizan con una limpia intención de hallar la verdad, pero suele aparecer su mente menguada; sus vasos son pequeños, y no quieren que les sean rebalsados. La llamada plebe teje, por el contrario, el poema en torno de los que fueron mejores que ella; está muy desposeída y, sin embargo, no conoce envidia y aumenta su material de adoración. Está en ellos menos empañada la memoria de lo divino y cuando encuentran algo semejante lo hospedan fácilmente.

Una leyenda es ésta:

Vinieron a la madre los dolores del parto y su sufrimiento se prolongaba contra la naturaleza. Pica se revolvía en el lecho entre lamentos. Podría decirse que la carne se negaba a entregar a ese que la superaría. Entonces golpeó a la puerta un peregrino y dijo que la madre no daría a luz mientras no se la sacase de su lecho suntuoso, y se la transportase al establo de la casa.

Así se hizo, se la puso en el heno pisoteado entre las vacas que mugían mirando la agitación del nacimiento, y los asnos que miraban a la enferma con sus grandes ojos negros.

La otra leyenda es la del bautizo del niño.

Estaba todo preparado y la comitiva brillante ya iba a salir, cuando golpeó al portal un segundo peregrino, más polvo y vejez que vestidos. Dijo que quería sostener la cabeza del recién nacido en la pila bautismal.

Volvió a aceptar Pica, que viene a ser obediente a la Gracia, como la otra Madre, y el cuerpecito fue sostenido por el vagabundo, entre el asombro de los burgueses que vieron aguada su fiesta con semejante presencia.

La Iglesia no defiende la autenticidad de los dos relatos, la dan los biógrafos sólo por conceder sitio a estos dos frescos candorosos. Están bien en la puerta de una vida que la ingenuidad humedece, en cada episodio, como un largo rocío.

México, 1923

HAIR

The hair on St. Francis's head was but a light breeze across his temples.

The mother nurtures the child with all of her feelings. She strengthens his body's little skeleton, employing all of her immense will to love; she softens his flesh with her tenderness; his hair is fashioned with daydreams. When Francis's mother prayed, she would play with the golden beauty of his little head. So did she make her prayer more delicate and light.

When Francis was a boy and women loved him, his hair didn't tempt them. It wasn't twisted and charred with that Italian curliness that resembles tough grass and is full of energy. Nor were his locks reddish, forming a flame around his neck, looking like the red sun on the Italian plains. It was that imperceptible gold of the lawn that dries out before going to seed. It seemed an omen of that sweetness already arising from deep within his heart.

LOS CABELLOS

Los cabellos de San Francisco eran no más que un vientecillo en las sienes.

La madre cuaja al niño con todas sus emociones. Le endurece la armazoncilla del cuerpo con su tremenda voluntad de amor; le hace las carnes blandas con su ternura; los cabellos se los hace con ensueños. Cuando la madre de Francisco rezaba, iba jugando con el bello dorado de su cabecita. Así se le hacia la oración más delicada y ligera.

Cuando Francisco fue mozo y las mujeres le amaron, sus cabellos no las tentaban. No eran duros y quemados con esa ensortijadura italiana que se parece a las yerbas más tercas y que está llena de energía. No eran tampoco rojizos para cuajarle una llama en torno del cuello, haciendo como visible el sol rojo de las llanuras italianas. Eran de aquel dorado imperceptible del césped que se seca antes de madurar, y parecían el anuncio de aquella dulzura que ya venía subiéndole a su corazón.

México, antes de junio 1923

EYES

And what would St. Francis's eyes have been like? They were like the flower's center, always moist with tenderness.

The smoothness sometimes found in the sky welled up in them; their depths were softened by love. He found it hard to shut them when night fell over the countryside after he had kissed the world with his gaze from early in the morning.

Sometimes they didn't let him walk. They would light on some pool or flowering branch like a child at the maternal breast. They ached with tenderness, they ached with love . . .

LOS OJOS

¿Y cómo serían los ojos de San Francisco? Estaban como la hondura de la flor, mojados siempre de ternura.

Habían recogido las suavidades que tienen algunos cielos; el fondo de ellos estaba mullido de amor. Le costaba cerrarlos sobre el campo cuando anochecía, después de haber besado el mundo con la mirada desde la primera mañana.

A veces no le dejaban caminar: se prendían en un remanso o en una rama florida, como el hijo al pecho materno. Le dolían de tiernos, le dolían de amor...

México, antes de junio 1923

VOICE

How would St. Francis have spoken? Imagine his words, sweetness dripping from them, like juice from fruit! Imagine hearing them when the air was full of dry echoes like a shriveled thistle! The voice of St. Francis made the landscape turn toward him like a face: it made the tree sap quicken with love and rise, and it made the rose, lazy with sweetness, unfurl its whorl of pleats.

It was a still, small song, like water running under fine-grained sand. And Francis sang his songs with that accent muffled by humility. (More than words, song requires a shivering of the voice.)

St. Francis's speech slipped invisibly into people's ears. Deep within them, it became a handful of the smoothest flowers. People didn't understand what that strange smoothness did to them. They didn't know that words are invisible garlands unfurled within the body's depths.

The miracle of his voice was even greater than that of his hands.

Sometimes Francis didn't touch the breasts of lepers. He spoke to them, hands folded, and his breath was the real ointment that poured forth, relieving the sore.

And Francis became a mouthpiece for songs, so that he would become a mouthpiece, perfect, for the greatest love. Unlike Pascal, he didn't want to search for God by moaning in the darkness. He sought the Lord in the throbbing of his joyful songs like the living pulse of golden motes in a ray of sunlight.

"What is the greatest sweetness that you have achieved in the world below?" angels would ask the Lord. And the Lord answered them:

"The prize wouldn't go to honeycombs; it goes to the ever-ready lips of my servant Francis, the singer."

LA VOZ

¡Cómo hablaría San Francisco! ¡Quién oyera sus palabras, goteando como un fruto, de dulzura! ¡Quién las oyera cuando el aire está lleno de resonancias secas, como un cardo muerto! Esa voz de San Francisco hacía volverse el paisaje sobre él, como un semblante; apresuraba de amor la savia en los árboles y hacía aflojar de dulzura su abullonado a la rosa.

Era un canto quedo, como el que tiene el agua cuando corre bajo la arenita menuda. Y cantaba Francisco sus canciones con ese acento amortiguado por la humildad. (Cantar es tener un estremecimiento más que una palabra en la voz.)

El hablar de San Francisco se deslizaba, invisible, por los oídos de los hombres. Y se hacía en sus entrañas un puñado de flores suavísimas. No entendían los hombres aquella suavidad extraña que les hacía. Ignoran que las palabras son guirnaldas invisibles que se descuelgan hacia las entrañas.

Hasta era mayor que el de las manos este milagro de la voz.

Francisco no tocaba a veces el pecho de los leprosos. Les hablaba con sus manos cogidas, y el aliento era el verdadero aceite que resbalaba, aliviando la llaga.

Y se hizo Francisco boca de canciones, para ser boca de suma bondad, boca perfecta. No quiso buscar al Señor con gemidos en la sombra, como Pascal. Lo buscó en el latido de sus canciones gozosas, semejantes al latido vivo de polvo dorado que hay en un rayo de sol.

"¿Cuál es la mayor dulzura que has alcanzado allá abajo?" solían preguntar los ángeles al Señor.

Y el Señor les respondía:

"No son los panales que se vencen: son los labios que están siempre bien henchidos de mi siervo Francisco cantador".

México, antes de junio 1923

HANDS

And his hands?

I tend to happen onto them on the underside of a leaf, which has a furry, ashen layer of down.

The saint's robe was dry and scratchy; his beard was like the robe; his cheek lightly peeling from the sun of Assisi, but because his sackcloth was scratchy and gray, he always held his hand out to those creatures in whom the memory of the divine becomes mildness and grace.

They lingered in the grass; they delighted in the lily, from the stem's base to the twisting petal. They rested upon lambs, delighting in the sensation, the touch.

A workingman's hands are always thrust into life's harsh labors. Unfamiliar with lotion, the backs were thick-skinned, yet the palms were acutely sensitive. Extended in a handshake, this palm was surprising . . . Even at the hour of rest, they lay, slightly cupped, as if cradling a flower or a tuft of fleece.

In the sores of the lepers, those hands weighed less than the gentlest of breezes.

Nature must work long and hard to develop such merciful hands! After Jesus, thirteen hundred years went by, weaving them. How much easier to produce the wide curve of the forehead, teeming with thought.

When pain spreads the net of humanity's aching viscera, the earth develops, again, another such pair of hands.

And I usually look for them among the crowds. For the present moment drips blood like a fisherman's net and the time has come for those hands to appear at the doors of our poor homes.

LAS MANOS

¿Y sus manos?

Yo he solido encontrarlas en el reverso de una hoja que tiene vello ceniciento y afelpado.

El sayal del santo era seco y áspero; su barba era como el sayal; la mejilla, estaba un poco despellejada del sol de Asís; mas, como era áspero y gris su sayal, él tenía siempre la mano extendida hacia aquellas criaturas en que la remembranza divina se vuelve suavidad y gracia.

Se quedaban en las hierbas mucho tiempo; gozaban bien al lirio, de la base hasta la torcedura del pétalo; se dormían sobre los corderillos por el deleite del tacto.

Pero siendo manos de varón de humildad que andaban metidas en las durezas de la vida y que no conocían óleos, siendo el dorso grueso, la palma era fina y sentidora. Al dar la mano, esta palma sorprendería... Aún cuando cayeran en la hora del descanso, se le quedaban esponjadas como si estuvieran siempre guardando una flor o un copo de lana.

En las llagas de los leprosos aquellas manos eran menos que un vientecillo, de livianas.

¡Cómo le cuesta a la naturaleza amasar tales manos para la misericordia!

Después de las de Jesús se demoró mil trescientos años en tejerlas. Con más facilidad hace la curva ancha de la frente para los pensamientos numerosos.

Cuando el dolor extiende ya como una red las vísceras padecedoras de los hombres, la tierra se pone a hacer otra vez estas manos.

Y yo suelo entre las multitudes buscarlas. Porque la hora, como red de pescador, gotea de sangre, y ya es tiempo de que vuelvan a asomar aquellas manos a las puertas de nuestras pobres casas.

México, antes de junio 1923

SICK

Francis became sick, and they asked him how he had been treating his body, he who freely gave away caresses above all else. That was when he confessed that he hadn't behaved well toward "Brother Ass." He begged forgiveness, smiling.

Yes, Pobrecillo! Everything under the sun has experienced your tenderness except for that body of yours, so close to you, within which your breath sounded as hollow as a reed . . .

Your neglect began when you left your home, with its purple, with its fine-tasting delicacies. You even felt a little resentful, for it had enjoyed much.

You didn't give your temples, in all their delicacy, a fleecy little pillow all puffed up for you. You didn't stretch it out on a soft mattress, where the boniness of its joints wouldn't be felt. You didn't pamper it with the earth's fine oils; and if from time to time you gave it some fruit, you sought out the least sensual, the least delightful ones. It moaned with fatigue and you didn't want to hear it; you passed by the shaded gardens. Using the excuse of your love for Brother Sun, you let it be scorched like a sheath of a green pea.

Because the cave's dampness didn't agree with you, you stayed there like a pool of penance. You even flogged it uselessly: your slender flesh had already let your instincts fall away, dead.

You treated it as a stepfather treats his tender little child. You lay awake, fearing that it was preparing to trap you, which you abhorred. That was thankless. The only place where you let it climb was in the trills of birdsong.

And it was very hard, Francis: you could move through the body as if spellbound, under the light's ineffable veil, and feel brother wind slapping you . . .

You say that you will mend your ways, but you didn't want to love what God set closest to you. That is why the only thing from which you withheld tenderness will fold up forever.

ENFERMO

Enfermó Francisco, y le preguntaron cómo había tratado su cuerpo, él que repartió caricias sobre todas las cosas. Entonces confesó que no se había portado muy bien con el hermano Asno, y le pidió perdón sonriendo.

¡Sí, Pobrecillo! Toda la materia derramada en la luz te conoció la ternura, menos ese tu cuerpo tan apegadito a ti, dentro del cual sonaba como dentro de un junquillo tu aliento...

Desde que dejaste tu casa, donde tuvo púrpura y saboreó manjares, comenzó tu desprecio; hasta le guardabas un poco de rencor porque había gozado mucho.

No le diste a tu sien, delicadísima, una almohadita del vellón del cordero que se esponjaba para ti también; no le tenías en un colchón blando, donde no se sintiera las coyunturas descarnadas; no le regalaste con los buenos aceites de la tierra; y si le dabas algunas veces frutas, buscabas las menos sensuales, las menos deleitosas. Te gemía de fatiga y no le querías oír; pasabas de largo por la sombra de los huertos. Con el pretexto de tu amor por el hermano sol, hiciste que lo quemara, como a la vaina de la arvejita.

La humedad de la gruta no le era grata, y lo dejabas en ella como en una piscina de penitencia. Hasta lo oprimiste con cilicios inútilmente; tu carne delgada ya había dejado caer los instintos, muertos.

Fuiste para él como un padrastro para su hijito tierno. Tanto velabas, de miedo que te tendiese una celada, que lo aborreciste. Fue una ingratitud. Sólo le concedías dejarse trepar por la saetita de un canto de pájaro.

Y fue mucha dureza, Francisco: por él pudiste andar como encantado, bajo el velo inefable de la luz, y sentir al hermano viento palmotearte...

Tú dices que te enmendarás; pero él va a doblarse para siempre, y así la cosa que Dios te puso más cerca fue la única que no te derritió de ternura y que no quisiste amar.

México, antes de junio 1923

CONVALESCENCE

Your new life begins in convalescence, Francis. An illness changes your soul and makes the past fall from you like a dry shell.

I remember, when I read about this, a point to which your biographer pays little heed: the convalescent's soul is in a sensitive state. Very rich with tenderness!

The blood has let go of its heaviness, and resembles a breeze coursing through the veins. The soul easily takes flight like a long-stemmed leaf that waves back and forth in the air. The soul's presence is more acute and the flesh lets itself be forgotten.

The eyes have grown wider, Francis; the forehead seems to become broader and whiter. We are so delicate that we hear the falling of a rose; we become so tender that the slightest perfume makes us drunk like a mountain of thick gardenias.

As strength disappears, so does cruelty, Francis. We aren't abrupt; we laugh and cry with a most exquisite refinement at the corners of our lips. We're a bit angelic, less human, and on that account, quite sweet.

LA CONVALECENCIA

Tu vida nueva empieza en una convalecencia, Francisco. Una enfermedad muda tu alma y te hace caer el pasado como una corteza seca.

Yo recuerdo, leyendo esta noticia a que tu biógrafo da poca importancia, que es fino estado de alma el del convaleciente. ¡Y muy rico de ternura!

La sangre se ha desprendido de su grosura, y se parece más a una brisa que fuese por las venas. Está el alma fácil para el vuelo como las hojas de largo pecíolo que se mecen mejor en el aire. El alma es más aguda presencia y la carne se deja olvidar.

Los ojos, Francisco, se han ensanchado; la frente se pone como más espaciosa y más blanca. Somos tan delicados que oímos el caer de una rosa; estamos tan enternecidos que un perfume insignificante nos embriaga como un montón de espesas gardenias.

Con la fuerza se nos ha ido la crueldad, Francisco. No somos bruscos; reímos y lloramos con una finura muy exquisita en el extremo de los labios. Somos un poco angélicos, menos hombres y por eso muy dulces.

México, antes de junio 1923

PRAISE

Francis, you didn't want to praise men because the Lord of all praise is One and one only. Praise things, yes: they don't grow proud. Since when does the lily shiver when its whiteness is described? But as for us . . . praise tickles our ears agreeably, swelling our chests in an ugly way.

So much are we given to praise that we seem, by contrast, like traders in colored beads, exchanging praise for praise . . . So do we move slowly toward perfection. If each of the lily's petals waited to be praised, the second petal would be much delayed in sprouting; if the babbling brook were waiting to be heard, it would remain at a standstill on the mountainside.

When we become stained with impurity, we are quick to hide it, but we exalt a sliver of virtue when it arises in us, hoping that the passerby will smile . . .

Instead of our hunger for praise, you had a hunger for humiliation that bordered on frenzy, my Pobrecillo. The soul, luminous as a dewy meadow, awoke in you one day, and you called out to a minor friar and you asked him to humiliate you by telling you a false litany of miserable things.

It was also due to your humility that you, Francis, unlike your brother friars, never liked to think that God made the creatures, the sheep, cows, and deer, to serve and glorify man. The creatures were born for themselves, which is why you call them sisters. Even in our prayers, we say that the stars illuminate the sky for our poor eyes, for us worms.

We are weak, Francis, like the hollow cane that needs the wind in order to be heard. You, little Francis, were strong, because when you sang, you didn't need to hear your song rolling over the hills in a wreath of echoes.

EL ELOGIO

Francisco, no querías alabar a los hombres porque es Uno solo el dueño de toda alabanza. A las cosas, sí, las alabanzas: ellas no se engríen. ¿Cuándo el lirio tiene un estremecimiento si se dice su blancura? Nosotros sí... El elogio nos hace un grato cosquilleo en los oídos; el pecho se nos hincha feamente.

Mucho alabamos en cambio nosotros, tanto que parecemos cambiadores de cuentas de colores, trocando alabanza por alabanza... Por eso andamos lentos en la perfección. Si el lirio a cada pétalo que echa esperase el elogio tardaría en echar el otro pétalo; si el agua cantarina aguardase que la oyesen se quedaría parada en la vertiente.

Cuando nos hacemos una mancha de impureza la ocultamos con ademán rápido; pero en cuanto nos nace una puntita de virtud la levantamos, esperando la sonrisa del que pasa...

En vez del hambre nuestra de alabanzas tú tenias un hambre de humillaciones que llegaba a parecer frenesí, mi Pobrecillo. Si un día te amanecía el alma luminosa como una pradera con rocío llamabas atribulado a un fraile menor y le pedías que te humillase diciéndote una letanía de miserias que eran mentira.

Tú, Francisco, por humildad también, no quisiste nunca pensar como los hermanos de tu fe que Dios hizo a las criaturas: corderos, vacas, venados para el servicio y gloria del hombre. Las criaturas nacieron para sí mismas, y por eso tú las llamabas hermanas. Nosotros decimos hasta en nuestras oraciones que las estrellas del cielo alumbran para nuestros pobres ojos de gusanillos.

Somos débiles, Francisco, como la caña que necesita del viento para oírse. Tú, el pequeño Francisco, eras fuerte, porque no necesitabas al cantar oír tu canto rodando por los cerros en un collar de ecos.

México, antes de junio 1923

NAMING THINGS

Francis, you had the gifts of choosing and singling out for praise. You loved the worthiest things. Walking the earth, you knew it through and through, but you chose the most beautiful creatures. In addition to the gift of steadfast love, which is the richest gift that we can receive, you were graced with the wit to name everything well.

Like Teresa [of Avila], your very subtle sister, you loved water. Sun, fire, and the earth's dark furrow are but sisters, three different beauties, each of them perfect.

Water is mystic like crystal: it forgets itself in the clear fountain. The pebbles and weeds look up from the water's bottom toward the sky, at the clouds, at the woman who is passing by, and the very humble water nearly vanishes. The water is a kind of St. Francis for the world in its joy and levity. The crazy child shapes a throat from the stone that is broken and starts singing through her. It is agile with that virtue which is elegance in heavy matter. And in its delicacy, it is livelier than the rough beasts. Wherever it manages to rest, it gazes long and deeply.

Your narrow body delighted in feeling the sun. It scattered across you like slender leaves. After the extended dampness of the cave you found it very tender—a little excessive but with the excessiveness of strong wine—in your long journeys through the Umbrian villages, it struck you as healthy, for drying the open wounds of the lepers and as quite childlike when it cast little golden disks over the water . . .

You enjoyed the feeling of a fire that burned just like the one within your breast. The small, dancing flames seemed to you like children skipping in a frenzied circle . . .

And like few lovers, you received the gift of knowing how to bestow names, precious names, on the world's creatures. Your adjective is marvelous, Francis: you call the fire "robust" and the water "humble and chaste."

The world's creatures loved you, Francis, not just for your saintliness but because they liked your naming them precisely, neither spoiling nor being stingy with them.

Your skills extend into many things as you settle an invalid at his bench with no feeling of poverty and you speak of things as they are, conveying joy with well-measured words.

Other saints weren't like that, Fancis. In their language with their lesser brothers, they were careless or disdainful. They took care only with the Lord's language. This, too, was part of your elegance, of your outstanding spirit. Not even in speaking with the furrows of the field could you be seen as coarse, my Pobrecillo.

Teach me this, too, Francis, which is another deep form of sweetness.

NOMBRAR LAS COSAS

Tú, Francisco, tenías don de selección y don de elogio. Tú amaste aquellas cosas que son las mejores; caminando por la tierra, todo lo conociste; pero elegías las criaturas más bellas. Y además del don del largo amor, que es el más rico de cuanto podemos recibir, te fue dado la gracia de saber nombrarlas donosamente.

Amaste el agua como Teresa, tu muy sutil hermana; el sol y el fuego, y el pardo surco de la tierra, tres bellezas diferentes, que sólo son hermanas por ser cada una perfecta.

El agua es mística como el cristal: se hace olvidar en la fuente clara, y las guijas y las vegetaciones del fondo miran el cielo, las nubes y la mujer que pasa, a través de la humildísima que se vuelve inexistente. El agua es una especie de San Francisco del mundo: es su alegría y su levedad. Hace, la loquilla, una garganta de piedra que se rompe y se pone a cantar en ella; es ágil: tiene esa virtud que es elegancia en la pesada materia. Y en su delgadez va más viva que los animales toscos. Donde cobra reposo se hace mirada, una profunda mirada.

Al sol lo gozaste bien por tu angostito cuerpo. Te traspasaba como a las hojas delgadas. Lo hallabas muy tierno después de la larga humedad de la gruta; era un poco excesivo, pero con el exceso del vino generoso, en tus jornadas largas por los pueblos de la Umbría, te parecía salutífero secando las llagas descubiertas de los leprosos, y muy niño cuando hace en el agua lentejitas de oro...

Te gustaba sentir el fuego encendido lo mismo que el de tu pecho. Las pequeñas llamas triscadoras te parecían niños saltando en una ronda de frenesí...

Y como a pocos amantes te fue dado *el saber nombrar*, de precioso nombre, a las criaturas. Tu adjetivo es maravilloso, Francisco: llamas robusto al fuego, humilde y casta al agua.

Las criaturas te amaban no sólo por tu santidad, Francisco, sino por que gustan del que las nombra justamente, sin abundancia de mimos, pero sin mezquindad.

Hábil tú para muchas cosas: para acomodar a un llagado en un banquito sin que sintiese su pobreza y para decirle a las cosas lo que son, dándoles alegría, con la palabra bien ajustada.

Otros santos no eran así, Francisco: descuidaban o desdeñaban su lenguaje con sus hermanos inferiores, cuidando sólo el del Señor. También era esto parte de tu elegancia, de tu gallo espíritu. Ni conversando con los surcos del campo te pudieron ver burdo, mi Pobrecillo.

Has de enseñarme esto también, Francisco, que es otra forma profunda de dulzura.

México, antes de junio 1923

VESSEL

Francis, you were carving a vessel from a scrap of wood.

As you had so often studied the shapes of flowers and the world, which is also a cup, you were making the vessel beautifully. How agile were those fingers of yours, brother, and what a free-handed carving into the fresh wood! But the hour for prayers came, and the trance of the happy task kept you at work while you were praying, with the words falling with a slight carelessness from your lips, my Pobrecillo. The cup absorbed your gaze; your hand grew warm in striking the curved bowl, which became all the more beautiful. Then, as you came to the great word of the Psalm, you seemed to suddenly come to your senses. You realized that your voice was ragged and tepid in praise. You sense the devil luring you from your own work, tempting you with beauty, an immense temptation, and you threw your vessel into the nearest fire.

How beautiful it would have been, had your fingerprints remained on that wood, where you might have carved the leaf of a lily or an acacia! We who have followed in our love for you, century after century, would have sipped the water from the springs of Assisi in that bowl, into which you had set something like the flavor of your very heart. It was a slender vessel, made of a mere branch, and we would exalt it as we would your body. It would be polished and shine with our countless kisses. The woodcarvers have their patron saint: "Francis the Woodcarver," and those who can't sense the grace of your hymns would have seen it collected in the walls of that vessel. But you threw it into the fire, Pobrecillo, because you feared the devil of beauty taking charge of your soul.

You did well, Francis, because the Lord changed you to expand only the perfect cup of your prayer, and in that cup millions of souls would be bathed in grace.

And you did well to banish it quickly from your sight. The beauty of the work, Francis, grabs its creator like an octopus that lovingly strangles its cup or its verse. People have many vessels to set on their table, but the Lord is without praise at morning's rise and at the close of the night.

EL VASO

Tú estabas, Francisco, haciendo un vaso con un pedacito de leña.

Como habías mirado tanto las formas de las flores, y el mundo, que también es una copa, ibas haciendo el vaso con mucha hermosura. ¡Qué dedos tan ágiles los tuyos, frailecillo, y qué corte tan espontáneo sobre la madera fresca! Pero era la hora de los rezos y la embriaguez de la faena feliz te hizo seguir labrando a la par que rezabas, y la oración te caía un poco descuidada de los labios, mi Pobrecillo. El vaso te sorbía la mirada; la mano se te pegaba con ardor al cuenco, que iba haciéndose más y más hermoso. Entonces, al llegar a una palabra grande del salmo, fue como que despertaras. Te diste cuenta de que tu voz era desflecada y tibia en la alabanza. Sentiste que el demonio estaba haciéndote guiños desde tu propia obra, tentándote con la belleza, que es la tremenda tentación, y arrojaste tu vaso en la llama próxima.

¡Qué hermoso hubiera sido conservar la huella de tus dedos en ese leño, donde tal vez tallaste una hoja de lirio o de acacia! Los que hemos venido después amándote, siglo tras siglo, habríamos bebido el agua de las vertientes de Asís en ese cuenco que le habría puesto como el sabor de tu mismo corazón. Era un vaso ligero, hecho con una rama no más, y lo alzaríamos como a tu cuerpo. Estaría pulido y abrillantado de nuestros besos innumerables. Los talladores tuvieran su patrono: "Francisco, el Tallador", y los que no saben ver la gracia de tus himnos, la habrían visto cuajada en el costado de ese vaso. Pero lo echaste al fuego, Pobrecillo, porque tuviste miedo de que se apoderara de tu alma el demonio de la belleza.

Hiciste bien, Francisco, porque el Señor te había puesto a hinchar solamente el vaso de tu plegaria que era perfecto, y en ese vaso se debían bañar de gracia millones de almas.

E hiciste bien en hacerlo desaparecer rápidamente de tus ojos. La belleza de la obra, Francisco, coge como un pulpo a su creador, lo aprieta con enamoramiento a su copa o a su verso. Y los hombres tienen muchos vasos que poner a su mesa; pero el Señor está sin alabanzas cuando sube la mañana o baja la noche.

México, antes de junio 1923

FEET

The roads still remember them, as the face remembers a caress.

For St. Francis always traveled on foot. Humanity's pain, he thought, is scattered throughout the world, and so it should be searched out.

The feet of the Pobrecillo were as nervous and sensitive as wild grass, which because of the way the light hit them, seemed to move without wind. Their color was like poplar leaves that turn pale and rosy-edged with autumn; they were as agile as if they were stemmed like leaves.

Only when he walked through the cities did he wear a scrap of sandal under his soles. Traveling through the countryside, his feet went bare, kissing this land that is also God's face.

On coming to a creek, he left them to the water, which sang over his toes as with pebbles. Then he dried them in the sun, and this tender heat made them feel like little birds. He loved his nails, which are a tiny enamel for the flesh, and he trimmed them with that grace that he used in snipping dried growth from the rosebushes.

His feet bore the scent of wild grasses, of the fields of medicinal herbs, or of grain, revealing which Italian roads he had traveled. In the afternoon, sweetened by the memory, the grass would moan, "Now where will the Pobrecillo go off to? He was the only one to travel through without trampling us." He thought that the excellence of hands comes from their touching without touching, imperceptible as breathing, and that soles glide across the world. He thought, too, about how the earth's lord leaves no footprint, and that we sink too deeply into its lawns . . . So did he wander across this world as if it were a borrowed and priceless tapestry.

Kneading his lean feet, he might have told them: these are the least of the soul's servants; they are a gift from my Lord and they carry the soul to answer errands of mercy.

LOS PIES

Los caminos se acuerdan de ellos todavía, como se acuerda la frente de una caricia.

Porque San Francisco iba siempre de camino. El dolor de los hombres, pensaba, está esparcido por el mundo y hay que ir buscándolo.

Los pies del Pobrecillo eran nerviosos y estaban vivos como esas yerbas que, por un toque de luz en el ápice, parecen moverse sin viento. Por el color se parecían a aquellas hojas del álamo que el otoño hace transparentes y sonrosa en las puntas; y por lo ágiles, eran como si también tuviesen pecíolos como una hoja.

Sólo cuando caminaba por las ciudades llevaba el pedacito de las sandalias bajo de las plantas; si atravesaba el campo, iban desnudas, besando esta tierra, que es también el rostro de Dios.

Al llegar a un arroyo, los abandonaba en el agua, que cantaba en sus dedos como en las guijas. Después se secaban al sol y este calor tierno, se los hacía sentir como pajarillos. Amaba sus uñas que son como el esmaltillo de la carne y las cortaba con esa gracia con que iba despuntando el extremo seco de los rosales.

Iban en sus pies los olores de las yerbas y por ellos se conocía qué caminos italianos habrían atravesado. Campos de yerbas buenas o de cebadas. Las yerbas solían gemir en la tarde dulcísima por su recuerdo: "¿Por dónde andará ahora el pobrecillo? Sólo él atraviesa sin doblarnos". Y es que pensaba que la excelencia de las manos está en que toquen sin tocar, como el aliento, y la de las plantas en que resbalen sobre el mundo. Y pensaba también que el dueño de la tierra no la huella, y que nosotros le hundimos demasiado sus céspedes... Y así iba él por el tapiz de este mundo, como si fuese prestado y precioso.

Acariciando sus pies enjutos, tal vez les decía: Éstos son los servidores menuditos del alma; se los dio mi Señor y la llevan con diligencia hacia donde la está llamando la misericordia.

México, antes de oct. 1923

CAUTERY

They don't know what to do about your illness, Francis, and because your medieval men are barbarians, they are going put a red hot iron on your temples.

Your temples are thin, like those membranes that cover fruit, and they are sensitive despite the stone that has been your headboard. The wonder of your penance has been this: the sensitivity didn't grow dull in your vibrant body, sensitive to the light, sensitive to the shade. And they are going to bring a red hot needle to those childlike temples!

Then you make a request, full of aching grace, to Brother Fire:

"You were noble," you say, "and I have been good for you. Don't burn me more than I can bear."

You speak to the fire as to a living creature. You don't beg the doctor, who is less moved than the crackling brand.

And they draw the iron near; it grates in your flesh with the sound of the cicadas rubbing and creaking. . . . The fire bites you with the bite of a handful of vipers. Brother Fire hasn't recognized you and is eating away at your flesh.

But you don't leave with bad feelings, Francis, and you say that you felt no pain at all, to avoid shaming him . . .

There is no way, my Pobrecillo, that a moan would jump from your mouth, betraying you.

But Brother Fire should be cursed in spite of you because he didn't recognize your temples. He is like men, blinded by his own flame . . .

EL CAUTERIO

No saben qué hacer con tu mal, Francisco, y como son bárbaros tus hombres medievales, van a ponerte un hierro hecho brasa sobre las sienes.

Tus sienes son finas, como esas membranitas que cubren los frutos, y las tienes sensibles a pesar de la piedra que ha sido tu cabecera. La maravilla de tu penitencia ha sido esa: que no endureciera la sensibilidad en tu cuerpo vibrador, sensible a la luz, sensible a la sombra. ¡Y a las sienes de infante van a allegarte el punzón enrojecido!

Entonces tú haces un pedido lleno de gracia dolorosa al hermano fuego:

"Tú eras noble", le dices, "y yo he sido bueno para ti. No me quemes más de lo que puedo sufrir".

Le hablas como a criatura viva. No le ruegas al médico, menos conmovido que el tizón crepitante.

Y te allegan el hierro; te chirría en la carne con el ruido de las cigarras cuando frotan muchos élitros... Te muerde el fuego con una mordedura de un puñado de víboras. El hermano fuego no te ha reconocido y te está comiendo la carne.

Pero tú no le dejas mal, Francisco, y dices que no has sentido dolor alguno, por no avergonzarlo...

No hay manera, mi Pobrecillo, de que te salte de la boca el gemido, haciéndote traición.

Mas, el hermano fuego ha de quedar maldito, a pesar tuyo porque no te reconoció las sienes. Se parece a los hombres en que está ciego de su misma llama...

México, antes de oct. 1923

LEARN TO LOSE

Francis, you who achieved lasting joy, teach it to me. My soul is like the olive tree, standing joyfully, all brilliant and green, and when a little breeze tosses its leaves, its color turns ashen.

"Learn to lose," says Francis.

Teach me the easy joy that comes from looking at the open sky, the joy that costs nothing because it comes from a passing breeze; the joy of seeing the dawn, of looking at how the rose on the hillside grows in the morning in a few silent moments, looking at how the rawness of noon softens into the tenderest lavender of evening and how night thickens into a deep blanket of felt becoming dense, very dense.

"That is not all. Learn to lose," says Francis.

"Teach me," I repeat as if drunk, "teach me the naive joy that comes from feeling the water running between my fingers, my hand plunged into the river, the naive joy that bursts into a fresh laugh because a butterfly, so wildly painted as to seem a hallucination, lands on our feet."

"It is not enough. Learn to lose," says Francis.

"Teach me," I press on, "this durable joy, which comes from immense beauty that doesn't wear us out and from that small beauty that doesn't leave us unmoved. I want the face that I love not to wear me down, the book that I read not to become routine. And let me find beauty in the small objects that surround me: the cup, clear as a lily in which I drink my milk, this pot of tender leaves that grows throughout my day, this living lamp that shines over me."

"That isn't enough, either. Learn to lose," says Francis. And he keeps telling me: "Learn to lose your soft bed, but without the rough pallet hurting your ribs. Learn to lose the humanized shade of your hallway without being hurt by going out naked into the night. Learn to lose the faces that surround you, lovers, and for whom death will come calling, looking to undo the lines in which its tenderness became visible. Learn to lose all the softness, not just of life, but of God, whose service will suddenly seem as harsh as a nail file. Learn to lose your own blood, and joyfully let pus form in your sores, to lose your healthy breath and your sturdy heartbeat that is going to slow down or go crazy, and the burnt shade of your hair when the infinite ash of death descends.

"And once you have learned to lose, you will have achieved lasting joy, and then the color of your soul won't change like the leaves of the olive tree twisted in the wind."

Oh, Pobrecillo! I still don't know how to lose: in each theft I feel robbed and my arm rises in anger to recover the loss. I don't know how to lose! I don't know how to lose!

APRENDE A PERDER

Tú, que alcanzaste la alegría durable, Francisco, enséñamela. Mi alma se parece al olivo, que entero está alegre y brillante y cuando un vientecillo le vuelca las hojas, se queda con color de ceniza.

"Aprende a perder", dice Francisco.

Enséñame la fácil alegría que baja sólo con mirar el cielo abierto, la alegría que nada cuesta porque va pasando en el viento: alegría de ver amanecer, mirando cómo crece la rosa de la mañana en unos instantes de silencio sobre la colina, mirando cómo la crudeza del mediodía va suavizándose hasta tener las violetas tan tiernas de la tarde y cómo la noche se va espesando en una felpa profunda hasta ser densa, densa.

"Eso no es todo. Aprende a perder", dice Francisco.

"Enséñame", repito como embriagada, "la ingenua alegría, la que viene de sentir el agua correr entre los dedos, con la mano sumida en el arroyo, la que revienta en una risa fresca porque se posa en nuestros pies una mariposa tan pintada que alucina".

"No basta, aprende a perder", dice Francisco.

"Enséñame", continúo todavía, "aquella durable alegría que viene de que no nos canse la belleza grande, y que no nos conmueva la pequeña. Yo quiero que el rostro que amo no me fatigue, que el libro que leo no se me haga costumbre. Y hazme hallar hermosura en los menudos objetos que me rodean: la taza clara como un lirio donde bebo mi leche, esta maceta de hojitas tiernas que crece junto con mi día, esta lámpara tan viva que me alumbra".

"No basta tampoco eso. Aprende a perder", dice Francisco. Y sigue diciéndome: "Aprende a perder tu lecho blando sin que te duela el costado sobre el tosco jergón. Aprende a perder la sombra humanizada de tu corredor y que no te duela salir a la noche desnuda. Aprende a perder los rostros que te rodean, amantes, y por los cuales vendrá a llamar la muerte, para deshacer las líneas en que se hacía visible su ternura. Aprende a perder todas las suavidades de la vida y hasta la de Dios, cuyo servicio se te volverá de repente áspero como las limas. Aprende a perder tu propia sangre, y consiente con alegría que se haga pus en tus llagas; a perder tu sano aliento y el latido justo de tu corazón, que se va a retardar o enloquecer; y el color quemado de tus cabellos, cuando baje la ceniza innumerable de la muerte.

"Y cuando ya sepas perder, habrás conseguido la durable alegría, y entonces no mudará el color de tu alma, como el follaje del olivo que voltea el viento".

¡Ay, Pobrecillo! todavía no sé perder: me parece que me roban en cada despojo y se levanta mi brazo lleno de ira para recuperar. ¡No sé perder! ¡No sé perder!

México, antes de oct. 1923

LILY

Watching the petals open, "a lily," you said, "is Christ's face, or better yet, his cheek, turned toward the wind, as perfect as if it had been made for eternity and lasting no longer than a word in the wind. Brother Lily, you're teaching me to be perfect in the smallest of my actions, in those tiny actions that I tend to overlook."

"My Brother, the lily, always seems to be trembling. The sighs of the afflicted resound through the air, touching the petals. The lily is trembling because it is seen by the Lord, *and the lily feels that glance*. We don't feel it, which is why we're hard and proud."

"Brother Lily is white, not from pride, but to demonstrate whiteness. Without the lily and the snow, which falls late, the eyes would forget whiteness."

"It is silent, like all things, listening persistently since the first day of Creation. Pobrecillo, we stop hearing the murmur of the one who made us, for listening to our own chatter makes us drunk, and hardens our ears."

"If others hadn't been ready to spill out their many lies, the divine lesson is so simple that it could have reached us from the wild lily alone: existing in silence, feeling the pain that passes through the wind and slowly weaving whiteness from the heart into the petals."

And Brother Lily serves, believe it or not, by holding the dew so that it doesn't fall onto the ground. Holding it like a hand. And many creatures exist only to hold something. *So does Francis hold the Lord's words on his tongue almost weightlessly.*

EL LIRIO

"Un lirio", dirías tú mirándolo abrirse, "es el semblante de Cristo, o mejor, su mejilla puesta al viento. Es tan perfecto como si estuviese hecho para la eternidad, y dura lo que una palabra en el viento. Me estás enseñando, hermano lirio, que debo ser perfecto en mis pequeñas acciones, en esas menudillas acciones que yo suelo desdeñar".

"Mi hermanito lirio se halla siempre tembloroso. En el aire van pasando los suspiros de los afligidos y lo tocan sobre los pétalos. Y está tembloroso también porque es mirado del Señor, *y él siente la mirada.* Nosotros no la sentimos, y por eso estamos duros y erguidos".

"El hermano lirio es blanco, no por soberbia, sino para muestra de la blancura. Sin él y sin la nieve, que baja tardíamente, los ojos se olvidarán de ella".

"Está callado, y así están todas las cosas: siguen escuchando desde el primer día de la creación. Nosotros, Pobrecillo, dejamos de oír el murmullo del que nos hizo, porque nos embriagamos escuchando nuestra propia algarabía. Y ésta ha endurecido nuestros oídos".

"La divina lección es tan sencilla que nos hubiese venido sólo del lirio de las colinas, si no se hubiesen puesto otros a derramar su mentira numerosa: estar en silencio, sentir el dolor que pasa en el viento y tejerse la blancura lentamente del corazón hacia los pétalos".

Y el hermano lirio sirve, aunque no lo creas: tiene suspendido el rocío que así no cae en la tierra. Como una mano lo tiene suspenso. Y hay muchas criaturas que sólo existen para tener una cosa suspendida. *De este modo, Francisco sostiene las livianas palabras del Señor sobre la lengua.*

México, antes de julio 1923

DELICATENESS

A bee has entered a lily. The petals shake a bit and she penetrates the corolla. It makes a tiny sound, and the lily rocks. It was full of honey, and the pistil was heavy, laden with pollen. The bee goes off with its wings all wet and feet dripping. The lily remains whole and serene.

So do I want, Francis, to pass through things without bending a single petal, leaving only a sound within them and the smoothest memory that they held me.

LA DELICADEZA

Una abeja se ha entrado en un lirio. Se sacudieron un poco los pétalos y ella penetró en la corola. Hace un pequeño rumor, y el lirio se mece. Estaba lleno de miel, y con el peso del polen abundante en el pistilo. La abeja sale con las alas manchadas y las patitas goteantes. El lirio se queda íntegro y sereno.

Yo quiero, Francisco, pasar así por las cosas, sin doblarles un pétalo. Que quede sólo un rumor dentro de ellas, y la suavísima remembranza de que me tuvieron.

México, antes de junio 1923

PRESENCE IN THINGS

Francis, I tend to find you curled up in a sagebrush thicket . . . Luminous eyes shine from the depths and the tall branches move with the lurker. Then, gently, I part the branches and enter . . .

Occasionally shattering chestnuts that are the same color as your robe, it seems that you jump joyfully in a pirouette. You were imprisoned in the fruit so that the wind would rock you. You make a branch rock as softly as the sky, Francis.

In your playfulness, Francis, you have scattered "golden thimbles," wild poppies along the roadsides, so that walking has a bit of bewitchment in it.

You paint the spots on the pebbles. You are flecked with the divine like these seashells, coffee-colored like your clothes, flecked with white spots.

And what hand but yours has twirled these seashells, with your little finger playing inside them?

This flower's crown, with its long, curling tube, won't you blow on it, like a child with a goblet?

Weren't you the one who painted the tortoise's shell? It was the color of old wax, and you painted dark and light streaks across it.

And when the lake's surface ripples on a windless day, aren't you passing over it with your long robe? The boats crowd together on the shore, bumping as if they were talking to one another about it.

And the mosses, Francis: in touching the stones with your breast, you produce and shelter the moss so that the tree trunks grow tender, and they nurture this green and gathered wool where the dew sleeps.

Francis, a heretical doctrine tells of millions of elves. Because of their patience, shaping the finer things in the Creation was assigned to them.

I would willingly believe that you have existed from the very beginning of the world, Francis, and that you created crystal, the hail's tiny teeth, and the tiger lily's wild stripes.

Among the vast hierarchy of artisan gnomes, you would have been the Chief worker. You would snatch a bird and there, right before their eyes, with a quick flick of your fingers you would sketch out the wings. You would scale the trees and teach the elves to paint with clarity the very top of the crown, infused by light. So does the tree seem to be under a denser light.

Underneath the pines, you would sit with them and make a capsular model of a tiny, dark cathedral.

PRESENCIA EN LAS COSAS

Francisco, yo suelo encontrarte acurrucadito en un matorral de salvia... Unos ojitos ardientes brillan en el fondo y las ramas altas se mueven por el escondido. Entonces, junto con dulzura las ramas, y sigo...

A veces rompiendo las castañas del color de tu sayal, me parece que saltas alegre en una pirueta. Estabas prisionero en el fruto para que te meciera el viento. Da una rama, Francisco, una mecedura tan suave como la del cielo.

Tú jugando, Francisco, has hecho esta dedada de miel de los caminos y por eso el caminar tiene como un encantamiento.

Las piedrecillas pintadas las pintas tú. Y estas conchas de mar, café como tus vestidos, con pintas blancas, eres tú mismo jaspeado de lo divino.

¿Y qué mano sino la tuya ha podido dar vueltas y vueltas a estos caracoles de mar jugando con tu dedito adentro?

Esta corola de flor con tubito largo, ¿no la habrás estirado soplando como un niño desde el cáliz?

¿Y no le habrás pintado tú el caparazón a la tortuga? Lo tenía de color de cera vieja, y se lo veteaste de venas oscuras.

Y cuando la laguna se riza sin viento, ¿no vas tú pasando con tu sayal largo sobre ella? Las embarcaciones en la orilla se juntan, chocándose como si se lo contaran.

Y los musgos, Francisco, tú los cuajas tocando con tu pecho las piedras. Los troncos se ponen tiernos, y crían esa lana verde y ceñida, donde duerme el rocío.

Francisco, una doctrina herética, cuenta de millones de geniecillos. Se les encomienda, por pacientes, labrar las cosas finas de la Creación.

Yo creería de buena gana que tú existes desde el comienzo de la tierra, Francisco, y que has hecho los cristales, los dientecitos del granizo y las pintaduras del lirio atigrado.

Tú habrías sido como el Jefe de las inmensas jerarquías de gnomos artesanos. Cogerías un pájaro y delante de ellos le irías dibujando las alas con un toque rápido de los dedos. Treparías con los geniecillos los árboles y les enseñarías arriba a pintar de claro el extremo de la copa que se funde con la luz. El árbol, así, parece debajo, una luz más densa.

Te sentarías con ellos bajo los pinos a hacer el modelo de la cápsula que es una catedral diminuta y sombría.

México, antes de oct. 1923

FROSTBITTEN ROSE

Francis stopped in front of a plant and after caressing the flowers, he went on, touching a black knot, a leprous scar on the trunk and branches.

And when he found a broken branch, he cut a scrap from his robe to cover the wound so that the moisture wouldn't drain away.

One day, on a favorite rosebush, he discovered a rose that hadn't been able to open. It was frostbitten and had two petals pushed open like two tiny wings; the rest had gone hard.

"You poor thing," St. Francis said. "Brother Sun doesn't keep you warm enough. But you shouldn't lose the joy of opening, which is the happiest fate of being a rose. Because my breast drank deeply of Brother Sun, it is very warm, Sister Rose. Lie down here and we'll see if the hard bud loosens up."

The rose lay on Francis all throughout his siesta. One by one, she loosened her petals. With his head bent over the flower, he listens to the tiny noise that the flower's center makes when it swells and pops. Bit by bit, he sees the greenish-white turning to white-white.

So did Francis learn that when the last petal is about to loosen, the song of the flower is heard, the word of fullness. That word is so soft that hearing it requires a stopped pulse. It is the praise of the rose. A moment later, the oldest of the petals tumbles to the side, and the ineffable moment has passed.

The rose completed its circle and Francis sighed with joy.

The corolla was looking at him with the golden eye of its gathered stamens, and that day, he composed a song about the joy of opening, about a rose.

ROSA HELADA

Francisco se paraba delante de una planta y después de acariciarle las flores, iba tocando en el tronco y las ramillas un nudo negro, una cicatriz leprosa.

Y cuando encontraba una rama rota, se cortaba un pedacito del sayal para cubrirle la herida y que no se desangrara.

Un día halló en el rosal preferido una rosa que no podía abrirse. Le había caído escarcha y estaba con dos pétalos en alto como dos alitas abiertas; las demás se habían endurecido.

"Pobrecilla", le dijo San Francisco, "El hermano sol no te calienta lo bastante; pero tú no puedes perder la alegría de abrirte, que es toda la dicha de una rosa. De mucho beber al hermano sol con el pecho, llevo éste muy tibio, hermana rosa. Acuéstate aquí y veamos si se afloja el botoncillo duro".

Francisco tiene toda una siesta la rosa sobre sí. Ella va soltando los pétalos uno a uno. Teniendo doblada la cabeza sobre la flor, le escucha el pequeño ruido con que se hincha en el centro de cada pétalo y salta. Le ve ir mudando el blanco verdoso por el blanco-blanco.

Así aprende Francisco que cuando el último pétalo va a soltarse, se oye el canto de la flor, la palabra de la plenitud. Es tan suave esa palabra que hay que oírla parando los pulsos. Es la alabanza de la rosa. Un momento después el pétalo más maduro de abajo cae hacia un lado, y ha pasado el instante inefable.

La rosa redondeó su círculo y Francisco dio un suspiro gozoso.

La corola lo miraba con el ojo dorado de sus estambres amasados, y ese día, él compuso un canto sobre la alegría de abrirse, de una rosa.

México, antes de oct. 1923

THE LARK

You said that you loved the lark more than any other bird, for its flight straight to the sun. That was how you wanted our flight to be.

Albatrosses travel across the sea, drunk with salts and iodine. They're like loose waves playing in the air, never getting too far from the other waves. The blast of marine wind lifts them and to avoid losing momentum, they go no higher than the sea winds. Storks make long trips. They have cast the shadow of their flight over the face of the earth. But like the albatross, they fly along the horizon, resting on the hills.

Only the lark leaps from the furrow like a living dart and climbs, swallowed by the sky. Then the sky feels that the earth has risen. The heavy forests, which remain below, don't answer it. Nor does an answer come from the melodious rolling of the river or from the mountains, which are crucified upon the plains.

But a winged dart gathered its momentum and is singing, suspended between the sun and the world. Whether the bird has fallen from the sun or has arisen from the earth is unknown. Like a flame, it hangs between the two of them. When it has sung a lot, it falls, broken, into the wheat.

You, Francis, wanted us to fly up, straight up without the zigzag toward an immediate landing.

You wanted the morning air to be whizzing with the arrows of many freewheeling larks. You imagined, Francis, that a network of golden larks would float between the earth and the sky in each morning's praise.

We are heavy, Francis; we love our warm furrow, our routine. In our praise, we stand on tiptoes, as grass stretches up. The highest one reaches as far as and no farther than the tall pines.

Only at death do we fly straight up! Never again, like the heavy earth of the furrow, is our body added to our soul!

LA ALONDRA

Tú dijiste que amabas a la alondra por sobre todos los pájaros, por su vuelo recto hacia el sol. Así querías que fuese nuestro vuelo.

Los albatros se van sobre el mar, ebrios de las sales y de los yodos. Son como olas desprendidas, que juegan en el aire, sin soltarse demasiado de las otras olas. La ráfaga marina los alza y para no perder el impulso, ellos no van más alto que los vientos de mar. Las cigüeñas hacen largos viajes; han echado la sombra de su vuelo sobre el semblante de la tierra. Mas como los albatros, vuelan horizontalmente, descansando en las colinas.

Sólo la alondra salta del surco como un dardo vivo y sube, bebida por el cielo. Entonces el cielo siente que la tierra ha ascendido. No le responden las selvas pesadas, que quedan abajo. Las montañas crucificadas sobre los llanos tampoco responden, ni el rodar melodioso del río.

Pero una saeta con alas subió en su ímpetu y está cantando suspendida entre el sol y el mundo; no se sabe si el pájaro ha bajado del sol o ha subido de la tierra. Está entre los dos, como una llama. Cuando ha cantado mucho, cae, rota, sobre los trigos.

Tú, Francisco, querías que tuviéramos el vuelo vertical, sin el zig-zag, hacia las cosas donde nos posamos.

Tú querías que el aire de la mañana estuviese todo asaeteado por muchas alondras libres. Imaginabas, Francisco, que una red de alondras doradas flotase entre la tierra y el cielo en cada alabanza matinal.

Somos pesados, Francisco; amamos nuestro surco tibio; nuestra costumbre. Nos empinamos en la alabanza, como se empinan las hierbas. La más alta llega no más que hasta los pinos altos.

¡Sólo al morir tenemos el vuelo vertical! ¡Nunca más como tierra pesada de surco, se agregará nuestro cuerpo a nuestra alma!

México, antes de oct. 1923

THE CORD

The cord of your robe, Francis, is the Lord's arm that stretches across you from one side to the other. And since the little cord represents this embrace, you wanted it to be a pale, happy color, to stand out against the robe. Set in the middle of your body, you feel it all over, from head to toe. Sometimes you forget it; but on stooping to pick up a stone you feel it and remember.

Without the cord the wind would play freely with your robe, and you would feel yourself handed over to that smile of the land; because of the little cord, the robe doesn't flap all of a piece, and then you remember yourself. It doesn't wrap you too tightly: it lets blood circulate joyfully throughout your body; it lets you carry a coin for charity and bend over to wash lepers. The little white cord is full of grace. It resembles the pale bands of worms. It resembles some marks on flowers, which the Lord might have set as a sign by which to know them. All of us wear some form of clasp, Francis. For some, that cord is red, and it is called sensuality and it burns. In others, the little cord is greed and it squeezes the kidneys very hard. Others wear a light sash of songs.

Bit by bit I have been making a similar ribbon around myself. You are the clasp that I am slowly forming. It isn't perfect, not yet. Help me close it with your hand, skilled in tying. And tie the knot tight because I feel that I'm still slipping away from it. I want your white circumference to finish forming soon, to take possession of my life.

EL CORDÓN

El cordón de tu sayal, Francisco, es el brazo del Señor que va de tu costado a tu costado. Y como el cordoncillo representa ese abrazo, quisiste que fuera claro, de color alegre, y que se pintara bien sobre el sayal. Puesto en la mitad de tu cuerpo, lo sientes en todo él: en los pies como en la frente. A veces lo olvidas; pero al inclinarte a levantar una piedra lo sientes y te acuerdas.

Sin el cordón el viento jugaría con tu sayal libremente, y tú te sentirías entregado a esa risa de la tierra; por el cordoncillo, el sayal no se bate entero y entonces tú te acuerdas. No te ciñe demasiado: deja correr con gozo la sangre que riega tu cuerpo; deja que puedas cargar el asno de la limosna y doblarte a lavar a los leprosos. Es gracioso el cordoncillo blanco. Se parece a los anillos claros que tienen los gusanos. Se parece a algunas pintas de las flores, que también sean una señal que les puso el Señor para reconocerlas. Todos llevamos alguna ceñidura, Francisco. En unos el cordoncillo es rojo, y se llama sensualidad, y quema; en otros, el cordoncillo es la codicia y oprime demasiado los riñones. Otros llevan un cíngulo ligero de canciones.

Poco a poco yo me voy haciendo un cintillo semejante en torno mío. Eres tú la ceñidura que va cuajando con lentitud. Todavía no es perfecta. Ayúdame a cerrarla con tu mano hábil en ataduras. Y hazle un nudo firme porque siento que todavía me derramo fuera de él. Yo quiero que acabe pronto de cuajarse en tomo de mi vida, su círculo blanco.

México, 1923, o Italia, 1924

THE ROBE

Why did you make your robes that chestnut color, Francis? Maybe the wheat's burnt shafts gave it to you. They conceal the whitest flour swelling within them. So do you conceal sainthood . . .

But I believe, better yet, that you fell in love with that hue for its being colored like the rind of fruit. You wanted your robe to have this same humble color as the peel of fruit, its brothers.

Or maybe you chose it for being the color of the land, naked and much scorned but good for daily use.

You didn't want it tightly woven. You wanted it to feel like the remnants of wheat and straw in the colander. And you wanted it to be permeable, too, so that Brother Wind would filter in, playing with your body, and you wouldn't be too cut off from the light.

It was all patches, Francis! You would always be pulling its threads, using them to fix the wounded things you chanced across. When the bushes didn't recognize you, they would shred it to pieces . . .

Having it struck you as a kind of pride. You even wanted to be given one that had been used before, with dirty sweat from other bodies and the worsted wool thinned, whitened at the elbows and knees.

Sometimes they patched one together for you, using scraps from other robes. You wanted to feel that because you wore a body that God had loaned you, you would wear clothing that men loaned you.

If you had tossed it onto the hyena, sister to Gubbio's wolf, she would have become sleepy, feeling its tepid warmth spread over her back.

EL SAYAL

¿Por qué hiciste tu sayal de ese color de castaña, Francisco? Tal vez te lo dieron las espigas quemadas. Ellas disimulan la harina blanquísima que las hincha. Así tú disimulabas la santidad...

Pero creo yo mejor que tú te enamoraste de ese matiz por el color de la corteza de los frutos, deseaste para tu sayal este mismo color humilde que hay en la cascarilla de los hermanos frutos.

O tal vez lo elegiste por ser el color de la tierra, desnuda, el más desdeñado; pero que es bueno para el servicio cotidiano.

No te gustaba que lo tejieran con espesura. Querías sentírtelo como la pajuela volandera del trigo. Y lo querías también permeable para que el hermano viento entrara a jugar con tu cuerpo y no te separase mucho de la luz.

¡Tan remendado que lo tenías, Francisco! Andabas sacando siempre de él hebritas para liar las cosas heridas que encontrabas. Y también cuando los matorrales no te conocían, te arrancaban jirones...

Tenerlo entero te parecía una forma de soberbia. Y hasta quisiste que te lo dieran ya usado, con el feo sudor de los otros cuerpos, con la estameña blanquecina en los codos y en las rodillas.

A veces te lo hicieron con los restos de otros sayales. Querías sentir que, como llevabas prestado de Dios el cuerpo, llevabas prestada de los hombres la vestidura.

Si tú lo hubieses echado sobre la hiena, hermana del lobo de Gubbio, en el cubil se habría quedado como adormecida al sentirlo, tibio, sobre su lomo.

México, antes de oct. 1923

CHARITY

What we call "charity" means putting a big coin into an outstretched hand or paying for a hospital bed, Francis. Not you. When you gave, you gave of yourself.

You were familiar with leprosy and you would remain seated for hours on end, washing the rot. It was as if you were the very water and oil and the bandage, too.

You gave of yourself by way of the juicy fruit that you put into the mouth of the feverish person. You not only offered the monastery to friars; you gave of yourself in long patience. They tended to be great chatterers and they required tremendous patience. And when you threw some food at Gubbio's wolf, you also gave of yourself by stroking him along the neck while he ate.

And when you created songs you also gave of yourself absolutely, your heart afire.

And so, Francis, you wasted away, like the waning moon. You were already something like a joke of the flesh, for you talked and barely had a throat. Your hands thinned to the transparency of autumn leaves. Your flesh was a mirage of your former flesh. Your miracle was more real than your poor body. You had faded into the bas-relief of the land, and you were scarcely visible. Just like the waning moon.

You discover a hidden truth: we have nothing we can rightfully give except for ourselves. Everything else comes from the earth.

When you give away a harvest of fruit, it is the generous furrow of earth that does the giving. When we give away clothes, it is the laborious spinner who makes the gift. But when we give of ourselves, then yes, we truly give.

We give our surplus, Francis. We are so full; we grow somewhat tired of having our arms full of life's rich stalks of corn. We break the bags of golden wheat, and then we give so that we don't have to bend and gather what falls out. You gave and you gave and you gave yourself.

LA CARIDAD

Nosotros llamamos caridad a poner en la mano extendida una moneda grande, o a pagar una cama de hospital, Francisco. Tú no. Cuando dabas, eras tú mismo lo que dabas.

Conociste la lepra y te quedaste sentadito horas y horas lavando la podre. Parecía que eras tú mismo el agua y el aceite; y también la venda.

Te dabas tú en las frutas jugosas que ponías en la boca del calenturiento. A los frailes no sólo les ofrecías el convento; te dabas tú en paciencia larga. Solían ser muy charladores y necesitaban una gran paciencia. Y cuando echabas de comer al lobo de Gubbio, también te dabas tú con las caricias que le hacías en el cuello mientras comía.

Y cuando hacías canciones también te dabas tú todito, con tu corazón ardiendo.

Y por eso, Francisco, te gastaste como las lunas en su cuarto menguante. Eras ya como una broma de la carne, que hablaba y que ya apenas tenía garganta. Tus manos se adelgazaron hasta ser transparentes como la hoja de otoño. Tu carne era un espejismo de la vieja carne que tuviste; tu milagro tenía más realidad que tu pobre cuerpo. Te habías desteñido en el bajo relieve de la tierra, y apenas se te veía. Lo mismo que la luna en el cuarto menguante.

Tú descubriste una verdad escondida; que no tenemos derecho a dar sino a nosotros mismos. Las demás cosas son de la tierra.

Cuando regalamos cosecha de frutos, es el surco generoso el que da; y cuando regalamos vestidos, es el hilandero fatigado el que regala. Pero cuando nos damos a nosotros mismos, entonces sí, damos de verdad.

Nosotros, Francisco, entregamos lo que nos sobra. Estamos tan llenos, que nos cansamos un poco con la brazada de ricas mazorcas de la vida. Se nos rompen los sacos de oro del trigo, y entonces cedemos, por no doblarnos a recoger lo caído. Tú te diste, te diste, te diste.

México, antes de oct. 1923

THE NEIGHBORING CELL

You heard your brother say, "I'm coming from Francis's cell." And you called him, for him to answer, "Why do you say 'Francis's cell'? It isn't mine and from now on another brother will be occupying it."

Pobrecillo Francis, how it embarrassed you to own things! You have only this: a square meter of earth, of soil for silence, for solitude. And the earth is very large.

You need, Pobrecillo, a little bit of room in which to fit your bent knees and your body, stretched out to sleep, where your sigh takes flight, where they don't see you cry when you think that the hand of God has left you. Where they won't see you undressing yourself, removing the bloody sackcloth. Where the broad jokes of your brothers, who are somewhat rough, won't break the lily stem of meditation. Where your very animals leave you alone. Because the familiar sheep is used to walking around you, nudging you affectionately, and the wolf, turned into a monk, appears before you at every minute and distracts you with the burning coals of his eyes.

You need that piece of bare floor because if you stay outside in the courtyard of the monastery, a beautiful golden flower with four petals (perfect little flames), makes you lower your face and interrupts your prayer. And if you see the water running, you want to make songs.

I won't give up the cell, Francis, I need to get away from my brothers who are too caught up in their eagerness for the table, and whose tongues are always swollen and pouring, pouring out . . .

But you hand the cell over to your brother. You fear that once the lust for possession is kindled in your heart, it will never be appeased.

LA CELDA AJENA

Oíste decir a tu hermano: "Vengo de la celda de Francisco". Y le llamaste para replicarle: "¿Por qué dices su celda? No es mía y de aquí en adelante la ocupará otro hermano".

¡Pobrecillo Francisco, cómo te avergonzaba poseer! Tú tienes sólo eso: un cuadradito de tierra, un metro de suelo para el silencio, para la soledad. Y la tierra es muy grande.

Tú necesitas, Pobrecillo, un pedacito donde quepan tus rodillas hincadas y tu cuerpo extendido para el sueño, donde vuele tu suspiro; donde no te miren llorar, cuando te crees dejado de la mano de Dios; donde no te vean al desnudarte que sacas el cilicio con sangre y donde las bromas gruesas de tus hermanos, que son un poco burdos, no te quiebren el lirio espigado de la meditación; donde tus mismos animalitos te dejen solo. Porque la oveja familiar está acostumbrada a andar dándote topaditas cariñosas y el lobo, vuelto fraile, se te pone en la frente a cada instante y te distrae con sus ojos de brasas.

Tú necesitas ese pedazo de pavimento desnudo porque si te quedas fuera de él, en el patio del convento, una linda florecilla de oro que tiene cuatro pétalos (llamitas perfectas), te hace bajar el semblante y rompe tu rezo. Y si ves correr el agua, te dan ganas de hacer canciones.

Yo no renuncio a la celda, Francisco, necesito separarme de mis hermanos que están demasiado prendidos a sus afanes de la mesa, y que tienen la lengua siempre henchida, y la vierten y la vierten...

Pero tú entregas la celda a tu hermano. Temes que comience en tu pecho la lujuria de poseer, que no se aplaca nunca más.

México, antes de oct. 1923

NIGHT

Death also felt like gentleness, Francis. Everything must have been soft to you, touching your docile body.

How did you feel?

It approached you in utter quiet with silent heels and smooth gaze. It sat by your knees. You noticed how it arose from them, not feeling cold, but with a hint of chill like the slow creeping of rising pool water. It arose, numb, along your lean thighs. It came to your heart and like a fresh wave broke across it, stopping your breath. It drew and tightened a band around your throat, and the prayer's murmur sank into velvet. Its slender flour was dusting your open eyes. It seemed to you that Brother Sun was beginning to set, although evening made no sense, not at that hour.

It reached your hand, always cupped, caressing, and left it open. It fell bit by bit like multiple layers of felt over your ears, making the prayers of the monks alongside you feel distant. It stretched out the limbs that you had curled into bed, where you seemed as tiny as a child. At last it gave you what you had longed for: the loss of your body, which was sinking into the deep waters of the unconscious. And with a little shudder your soul let go, collecting from head to toe—as a flame collects in a tree trunk that burns through from both sides—in a lofty tongue of flame that arose, carried away.

And so did death treat you as a friend.

It couldn't betray you: nothing released from the hand of God spread over our heads, nothing in this world betrays us, Francis.

LA NOCHE

También sentiste la Muerte como una suavidad, Francisco. Al tocar tu cuerpo dócil, todas las cosas tenían que serte suavidad.

¿Cómo la sentiste?

Se te iba acercando muy callada, con talones de silencio y blanda mirada. Se sentó frente a tus rodillas; notaste como te subía por ellas, no un frío, una pequeña frescura como de agua de piscina que asciende, lenta. Te subió por los muslos descarnados insensiblemente; llegó al corazón, se derramó sobre él como una ola fresca, parándote el aliento. Te rodeó la garganta en una venda un poco apretada, y el murmullo de la oración se fue aterciopelando. Su harina delgada iba espolvoreándose en los ojos abiertos y te pareció que el hermano Sol bajaba al ocaso, aunque no cabía bien la tarde a esa hora.

Te extendió la mano siempre recogida por el hábito de la caricia y te la dejó abierta. Dejó caer, poco a poco, como muchas felpas espesas sobre los oídos, haciéndote lejano los rezos de los frailes que estaban a tu lado. Te estiró los miembros que recogías en el lecho, por parecer tan pequeñito como un niño. Te dio, por fin, lo que mucho habías anhelado: la pérdida del cuerpo, el cual se fue sumiendo en las aguas profundas de la inconsciencia. Y con un pequeño estremecimiento te desprendió el alma, recogiéndotela de la cabeza hasta la punta de los pies —como se recoge una llama en un tronco que arde horizontal— en una lengua alta que subió, arrebatada.

Y así te fue la muerte amiga.

No pudo traicionarte: ninguna cosa desprendida de las manos de Dios sobre nuestras cabezas nos traiciona en este mundo, Francisco.

La Coruña, España, enero 1925

PRECIOUS STONES

St. Francis died and his flesh mingled with the earth like the melted pulp from the fruits of autumn.

After him, there were many minor friars who also mingled with the loving land. And then men came by and the land remained after they had left, with the loneliness of its loving touches, its steep hills where Francis always sloped down into the warm bowl of the Umbrian valleys.

And when other beings came running along its slopes, playing, one day they discovered two precious stones in the clay of Assisi. They were the eyes of the Pobrecito.

From humility, his flesh wanted to dissolve and not remain intact like the cheeks of other saints. His skeleton, as thin as the veins of a leaf, also peeled apart quietly . . . But the eyes of St. Francis hardened into two stones of lights, round and lively.

The new men found them in a ridge of clay. They stared in amazement. The beauty of the old earth arose to their surface. In their reflection, they recognized the roses, the round white lambs, the birds, the roads. They turned them about and the whole earth passed through them . . .

This is how the world of forms, which had refused to be confined to weighty volumes of books, wants to remain within the two eyes that had best lived and walked through it.

The hard, shifting pebbles, the two pure opals, tossed and turned in a circle. And a strange tenderness took shape because of the dead creatures.

The only one that they didn't recognize was St. Francis, the owner of the marvelous diamonds. He had become as inexistent as water in the pool, and only showed himself, at every turn, to his brothers, the rose, the lily, the bees, the quail, the wolf and people . . .

LAS PIEDRAS PRECIOSAS

Murió San Francisco y sus carnes se mezclaron a la tierra como la pulpa fundida de las frutas de otoño.

Después de él existieron muchos frailes menores que también se mezclaron a la tierra amante. Y después pasaron los hombres y la tierra quedó sin ellos, con la soledad de sus caricias, de sus erguidas colinas que Francisco repechara haciendo siempre el cuenco tibio de los valles de Umbría.

Y cuando otros seres vinieron a correr por sus laderas, descubrieron un día, jugando, dos piedras preciosas en la arcilla de Asís. Eran los ojos del Pobrecillo.

Su carne por humildad, quiso disolverse, no quedo intacta como la mejilla de otros santos. Su esqueleto tan fino como nervadura de una hoja se desgranó también calladamente... Pero los ojos de San Francisco se endurecieron, para volverse dos piedras de luces, redonditas y vivas.

Los nuevos hombres las hallaron en la greda de una cuesta. Mirábanlas asombrados. A su superficie subía la belleza de la vieja tierra. Conocieron por su reflejo las rosas, los redondos corderillos blancos, los pájaros, los caminos. Hacíanlos girar y pasaba por ellos la tierra entera...

De esta manera el mundo de las formas que había rehusado quedar en los mamotretos sabios quiso quedarse en los dos ojos que mejor lo habían vivido caminando.

En corro, volteaban y volteaban las duras piedrecillas cambiantes, los dos ópalos puros. Y una ternura extraña se les hacía en el pecho por las criaturas muertas.

Sólo a San Francisco, el dueño de los diamantes maravillosos, no conocieron. Él se hizo inexistente como el agua en el remanso, y mostraba sólo, en cada vuelta, a sus hermanos, la rosa, el lirio, la abeja, la codorniz, el lobo y los hombres...

México, antes de oct. 1923

Roberto Montenegro, *Nubes y olas* (above) and *El astrónomo* (below)

CAPÍTULO 9

MÉXICO, 1923–1924

LIPS

And the lips of the Pobrecillo were slender; they were made for words as quick as lightning.

Everything has lips: those of the plowed furrow are thick, giving their fleshiness to the tubers and yielding oil to the black olive; the lips of the sea are wide and numerous and they spill over with that wild pleasure that makes the seagulls hoot. His could be forgotten, for they were almost always silent.

Their color wasn't passionate. I see them with that rosy pink color of budding jasmine.

Their smile persisted, even when sleeping, a smile distinct from ours, lacking the malice that was tucked away in the corners like a mustard seed.

They gave the land the gentlest kiss that it has received. As they had not kissed a woman's mouth, they knew no frenzy. His lips seemed small to him for kissing the world, and he began to sing songs. (Songs are like many lips spilled out among the creatures.) His smile uncovered the grace of his teeth, small, more delicate than ours, which squeeze tough meat.

And the breath knew no violent panting: it was like the almost imperceptible tremble of unmoving blades of grass.

Francis's lips were for made for compassionate song.

LOS LABIOS

Y eran delgados los labios del Pobrecillo; estaban hechos para las palabras ligeras como una exhalación.

Todas las cosas tienen labios: los del surco son espesas, tienen que dar su grosura a los tubérculos y entregar el óleo de la aceituna negra; los labios del mar son numerosos y anchos y derraman ese gozo salvaje que hace gritar a las gaviotas. Los suyos podían olvidarse porque estaban casi siempre silenciosos.

Su color no sería ardiente. Yo los veo con esa sonrosadura que tiene el jazmín en botón.

La sonrisa duraba en ellos hasta en el sueño, una sonrisa distinta de la nuestra, sin la malicia que se esconde como un granillo de mostaza en nuestras comisuras.

Ellos dieron a la tierra el beso más leve que ha recibido. Como no besaron boca de mujer, no conocieron frenesí. Le parecieron pequeños sus labios para besar el mundo, y se puso a cantar canciones. (Las canciones son como muchos labios derramados entre las criaturas.) Su sonrisa descubría la gracia de los dientes menudos, más delgados que los nuestros, que exprimen recias carnes.

Y el aliento no conoció el jadeo de la violencia: era como la tremolación imperceptible de la hierba quieta.

Le labraron a Francisco los labios para la canción con misericordia.

México, marzo 1924

THE SENSES
(DIALOGUES WITH ST. FRANCIS)

Francis, your brothers say that the five senses are vessels of impurity. They would like to break them.

"The eyes," they say, "come down to sip from the world, and sip so intimately that frenzy overtakes them. The sense of smell is demonic: it makes us steer clear of the house of the lepers when we pass along the road. The sense of touch is a rose that makes us dislike the sackcloth robe that we wear."

"Don't believe them, my daughter. The sense of taste makes heaven seem a table heaped with fruit for people who are crude. The sense of hearing makes a harsh voice strike your brothers as disagreeable, or so they conclude. But they're wrong, my daughter. I set my senses out to graze dutifully like white lambs. I lead my lambs through the sweet-smelling grass one morning, and when they desert me for other fields of clover because they want sweets, I make them return and I set them on a hard road. They wail for a bit, and then their bleating quiets down.

"Your eyes are beautiful, my daughter. God made their lids as fine as the little membrane that separates the seeds within the pomegranate. They're so childlike that they delight in the coloring of the leafy grapevine. At every moment they give you sips of joy. God wanted you to look at his many-hued land. How could you empty them?

"Your ears fill you with sounds and silences as nuanced as the seashells scattered across the beaches. Let them play with music, with the small murmured words of the earth, which never wants to remain quiet, and with the playful whispers in the air. You, daughter, are a vessel; don't turn away from the play of sound. Why should you break your ears?

"The senses wander the world as playfully as the light plays in trees. They know the world of things and emerge from it, pure.

"When you were a child, you played with paper kites. Oh, how you flew a kite far and high in order to feel the sky! The kite scaled the heights and was always yours, thanks to the little white string with which you controlled it. How far and deep did you raise it into the sky! It seemed like a bird and it slept in the wind. But it had the movement of your pulse and it was yours, yours! With it you happily pressed the sky. When it descended into your hands, it struck you as mysterious and even more beautiful.

"So is it with your senses, which are playful like kites, and they touch the divine in the land and they tremble and turn back on you as if bathed by the world's grace.

"I take care of my senses—take care of yours, too—for they could keep me pinned to the world like an ugly, crumpled kite."

LOS SENTIDOS
(DIÁLOGOS CON SAN FRANCISCO)

Francisco, dicen tus hermanos que los cinco sentidos son vasos de impureza. Querrían rompérselos. "Los ojos", dicen, "se bajan a libar las cosas, y las liban tan próximas a ellas, que les dan un frenesí. El olfato es demoníaco: nos hace esquivar la casa de los leprosos cuando pasamos por el camino. Y el tacto es una rosa que nos vuelve después ingratos el sayal sobre los costados".

"No les creas, hija mía. El gusto transporta para los groseros el cielo a una mesa alta de frutos. 'El oído', terminan, 'les vuelve odiosos a sus hermanos la voz áspera'. Se equivocan, hija mía. Como a borreguitos blancos, yo hago a mis sentidos pacer con obediencia. Yo llevo mis corderos por las hierbas olorosas una mañana, y cuando se me van, golosos, hacia otras manchas de trébol, los hago volver y los pongo sobre un camino duro. Me gimen unos instantes, después se apagan sus balidos.

"Tus ojos son hermosos, hija mía. Te los hizo Dios tan finos en los párpados como la membranilla que separa los dientes de la granada. Son tan niños, que gozan con las pintaduras de la hoja de la vid. Te están regalando a cada instante sorbos de alegría. Dios quiso que mirases su tierra coloreada. ¿Cómo vas a vaciártelos?

"Tus oídos se te llenan de ruidos y silencios matizados, como los que pueblan a los caracolillos de las playas. Déjalos jugar con músicas, con las palabritas de la Tierra, que nunca quiere estarse muda, y con los cuchicheos juguetones del aire. Tú, hija, eres un vaso; no te rehúses al juego de los sonidos. ¿Por qué habías de romperte tus oídos?

"Los sentidos andan jugando en el mundo como la luz juega en los árboles. Conocen las cosas y salen de ellas puros.

"Cuando niño jugabas con los cometas de papel. ¡Ay, cómo la encumbrabas para sentir el cielo! Subía la cometa hasta muy alto y era siempre tuya por el hilito blanco con que la movías. ¡Cómo la elevabas bien hondo en el cielo! Parecía un pájaro y se dormía en el viento. Pero tenía el temblor del pulso tuyo; y era tuya, ¡tuya! Pulsabas con ella el cielo alegremente. Cuando bajaba a tus manos, te parecía venir misteriosa y como más bella.

"Así andan ellos, tus sentidos, juguetones como las cometas, y tocan lo divino de la tierra y tiemblan, y vuelven hacia ti como bañados por la gracia del mundo.

"Yo cuidaba mis sentidos —cuídalos tú también— de que me quedasen prendidos en el mundo como una fea cometa hecha pedazos".

Oaxaca, México, marzo 1924

SLIVER OF NEW MOON

Looking at you, high in the sky, is the sliver of the new moon, soft as breathing. The sunset, which was sumptuous, goes on. The masterful tapestry of afternoon remains in the hills, but in the splendor of sunset the little sliver of moon is a drop of sweetness and my eyes turn to it and I smile at it. So, Francis, in God's heaven there are great saints like Paul, rich with passion, and like Augustine, rich as a golden sunset, and others who present a long and violent nightfall.

But my eyes have rested and want to remain in you, sliver of new moon, as thin as a strand of hair whose gold is lost in the blush.

And my wandering soul remains tied by your harmless knot.

LA LUNITA NUEVA

Está sobre el cielo, mirándote la luna nueva, tan leve como un aliento. Dura todavía el crepúsculo que fue suntuoso. Se demoran en las lomas los tapices magistrales de la tarde; pero en la esplendidez del crepúsculo la lunita nueva es una gota de dulzura y yo pongo mis ojos en ella y le sonrío. Así, Francisco, en el cielo del Señor, hay santos magníficos como Pablo, rico de pasión, y como Agustín, rico como un crepúsculo de oros, y otros que forman un ocaso grande y violento.

Mas mis ojos se han posado, y se quieren quedar, en ti, lunita nueva, tan delgada como un cabello de oro extraviado entre los arreboles.

Y mi alma vagabunda, queda atada por tu lazo que no duele.

México, 1924

FOOTSTOOLS

The Lord had two footstools, Francis: the earth was one, and the other was the human heart. His feet delighted in resting on the two footstools, innocent and bathed in grace.

When humanity was young, the pressure of those feet was crushing, as fruit is crushed.

They sinned, but their sin was less malicious than ours and the fear of God kept them shivering and pale as the tip of grass. They sinned like frisky deer and baby goats. They acted instinctively like the dense furrows in the ground, but like the furrows, they were always mild in God's hands. This made for tremendous stories.

But then this footstool broke, Francis. People invented freedom so that they wouldn't be footstools. Their sensuality became a sad, wrinkled lust. If they're pressed, the blood doesn't seep out like a pomegranate. They ooze with foul juice. And when they hate or are possessed by violence, they produce miserable screeches.

God has withdrawn His white foot from this footstool. But the Other one remains on the earth. Thus it flowers in spring, snow melts as the sun slices it, and the little animals burrow, violent, opening holes in the shrubs.

What you loved and what I love still bear the mark of His footprint.

These are the air, as fresh as a moist garland across the face; the fruit, replete with goodness, rainbow-colored when it blooms, marvelous and complete, or if it is dried and closed, it makes a good, wholesome food. There are the good, golden meadows that shine like the downy gold on the Earth's child-like head. There are little wild animals that run free as water and whose eyes gaze full of divine fear.

LOS ESCABELES

El Señor tenía dos escabeles, Francisco: uno era la tierra y otro el corazón de los hombres. Sus pies descansaban con gozo sobre los dos escabeles, inocentes y lavados de gracia.

Cuando los hombres eran nuevos se exprimían bajo la presión de aquellos pies, como se exprimen los frutos.

Pecaban, pero su pecado tenía menos malicia que el nuestro y el temor de Dios los mantenía como a las hierbas temblorosas y claras en el ápice. Pecaban como los ciervos y los cabritillos vivaces. Se ponían como los surcos densos de instinto; pero como los surcos eran siempre blandos en las manos de Dios. Contándole tenían grandes acentos.

Y este escabel se rompió, Francisco. Los hombres inventaron la libertad, para no ser escabeles. Su sensualidad se hizo una lascivia arrugada y triste. Si se los oprime, no revientan en una sangre como la granada: rezuman un humor impuro. Y cuando odian o tienen violencia, no rugen, dan chillidos miserables.

Dios ha retirado Su pie blanco de este escabel. Mas el Otro sigue puesto sobre la Tierra todavía. Así, ella florece en la primavera, fluye la nieve lacerada del sol y las bestiecitas abren violentas, los matorrales.

Lo que tú amabas y lo que yo amo son estas cosas que están todavía oprimidas por Su huella.

Son el aire, fresco como guirnalda mojada en la frente; son los frutos, tan llenos de donosura, pintados de todos colores, que si se abren, están intactos y maravillosos; y si se secan cerrados, dejan una pasta quemada llena de bondad; son los buenos pastos, que se doran como un vello sobre la cabecita niña de la Tierra; son los animalitos libres, que corren tan ágiles como el agua, y que miran con unos ojos llenos de divino miedo.

Oaxaca, México, marzo 1924

NET

This is a fisherman's net. It is golden and stretched out on the ground; it resembles a thick, dripping honeycomb moistening the sand. The fisherman pulls it up, steps into the boat, and heads off a bit into the lake.

Now he raises it, stretching it like a sail; now he lets it fall. He lowers it in silence to the depths. While the boat presses on, the net lies asleep at the bottom. Then, like a dream, I see it rise, full, and its weight is felt, marked in the muscles of the fisherman's arm.

That was what your word was like, Francis, golden like the net, without a brassy shine. So, too, in this silence so deeply buried in souls that it sometimes seems dead, inert. And after some days of having listened to you, men begin to shake and tremble, hoping to remain with you forever.

Then in your smile, the weight of your net became visible, Fisherman.

Like this net that is lying open on the beach right now, full of wildly beating flanks, your net catches souls of all colors, gray and violet, insignificant and splendid.

LA RED

Ésta es una red de pescador. Es dorada, y caída en el suelo parece una gruesa enmieladura que gotea, mojando la arena. El pescador la coge, entra en la barca, y se aleja un poco, lago adentro.

Ahora la alza, dándole impulso como de vuelo; ahora la deja caer. Baja hasta la hondura, en silencio. Mientras la barca cabecea, ella se está dormida en el fondo. Después, como un sueño, la veo subir cargada y siente su peso, que se marca en los músculos del brazo del pescador.

Así era tu palabra, Francisco, dorada como la red, sin brillo indiscreto. Así, con este silencio, se hundía en las almas y a veces parecía muerta en su fondo. Y después de unos días de haberte escuchado los hombres, volvían temblorosos, a quedarse contigo para siempre.

Entonces se veía el peso de tu red en la sonrisa tuya, Pescador.

Como ésta, ahora abierta en la playa y llena de costaditos palpitantes, tu red cogía a almas coloreadas, grises y violetas, insignificantes y espléndidas.

Oaxaca, México, marzo 1924

Roberto Montenegro, *San Francisco y la lepra*

CAPÍTULO 3

PARÍS Y PROVENZA, FRANCIA, 1926–1927

ST. FRANCIS'S CHILDHOOD: CHAPTER FROM A LIFE

Birth

Francis was born in Assisi in the month of September in 1182, probably on the 26th; it hasn't been possible to establish the precise day. We don't know, then, the day when this Francis, Lord of the Middle Ages, came into the world. We do know a lot about the bandits at the time and even about the aches and pains of this or that emperor.

His parents were Madonna Pica de Berlemont, who was born in or whose family came from Provence, and Pedro Morico Bernardone, a cloth merchant.

The order of his progenitors is deliberately inverted: Francis appears as no more or less than his mother's child. Bernardone is cited only in regard to some embarrassment.

The biographers agree in assigning a very comfortable situation to his parents. It is said that Madonna Pica had noble origins; for his part, the Merchant was pretty well-tanned from his travel throughout Italy and into France to develop the wealth of his household. In the town of Assisi, the family came to mingle with the aristocracy, for malice has always counseled people from noble lineages to show some goodwill and even some degree of fusion with rich semi-peasants.

There is talk of a wife who outdoes her husband in smooth manners and her heart's finesse, and of her less nobly born husband, a merchant who accommodates her out of gratitude.

Name

The child was given the name John; but he was called Francis when Bernardone returned.

The first name would have been more pleasing, transferred to Christianity from its religious meaning by the Baptist, who prepared the way, and by the Gospel, that red dahlia of the New Testament. But Bernardone didn't understand that a name is a profound thing, that a name presides over life and should be merged with our glance and with our gesture.

According to the commentators, Bernardone wanted to have in the boy a reminder of France, which had been his market. So he called him Francis, a name that must have been as strange back then as if we were to call a boy "Egypt" or "Ethiopia." Giving a new name to this truly new man was the only good that came of it. In Umbria, the word was known only through a road called The Way of Francis.

The child would be a road not for mules laden with cloth, but leading to Christ, and so long that it has circled the earth.

INFANCIA DE SAN FRANCISCO: CAPÍTULO DE UNA VIDA

Nacimiento

Francisco nace en Asís en el mes de septiembre de 1182, probablemente el día 26; no se ha podido establecer la fecha precisa. Ignoramos, pues, el día en que llegó al mundo este Francisco, Señor de la Edad Media, y sabemos muchísimas cosas de los bandoleros de su tiempo y hasta de los achaques que sufría tal o cual emperador.

Sus padres son Madona Pica de Berlemont, nacida en Provenza o descendiente de provenzales, y Pedro Morico, llamado el Bernardone, mercader en telas.

El orden de los progenitores se invierte voluntariamente: Francisco no aparecerá a través de su vida sino hijo de su madre; al Bernardone se le ha de citar sólo para alguna vergüenza.

Los biógrafos coinciden en asignar a los padres una situación holgadísima; se habla de que Madona Pica tenía origen noble; por su parte, el Mercader se había tostado bastante en muchas jornadas de Italia a Francia para hacer la riqueza de su casa. En la población de Asís la familia llega a mezclarse con la aristocracia, porque la malicia ha aconsejado siempre a las gentes de linaje cierta benevolencia y hasta alguna fusión con los semivillanos ricos.

Se habla de una esposa que aventaja al marido en suaves maneras y finura del corazón, y de un mercader complaciente hacia ella por esa especie de gratitud que se hace en el marido inferior.

El nombre

Fue dado al niño el nombre de Juan; pero el Bernardone a su regreso lo llamó Francisco.

Más grato hubiera sido el primer nombre, traspasado de sentido religioso para el cristianismo por el Bautista, que preparó los caminos y por el Evangelista, esa dalia roja del Nuevo Testamento. Pero Bernardone no entendía la cosa profunda que es un nombre, el nombre que preside la vida y que debe fundirse con nuestra mirada y con nuestro gesto.

Según los comentaristas, el Bernardone quiso tener en el niño un recuerdo de la Francia que había sido su mercado. Le llamó, pues, Francisco, nombre que en aquel tiempo debió extrañar tanto, tanto como si hoy llamáramos a un niño Egipcio o Abisinio. Una sola cosa feliz hubo en la ocurrencia: dar nombre nuevo a este verdadero hombre nuevo. La palabra era sólo conocida en la Umbría por un camino llamado Vía Francesca.

El niño sería un camino; pero no para los mulos cargados de telas sino un camino hacia Cristo, tan largo que ha ceñido la tierra.

Education

In marriage, there will always be two distinct criteria for judging many things despite the husband's relative benevolence toward the wife. There will be the perspective of the rowdy peasant who made a fortune and calls the shots, and there will be the woman with a better spiritual endowment . . . The conflict was evident in Francis's education. Pica wanted her son to become a well-read young man and round out a home that already had sufficient income. Bernardone, by contrast, wanted someone to build on his travels, to become knowledgeable in accounting, and to develop a foxlike eye for slippery business deals.

Pica simply stated her desire. She didn't fight with her husband. As a medieval wife, she had to be accepting once and for all.

Francis learned to read and write from the priests of the Order of St. George. He was an earnest student, keen for broad knowledge. His sensitivity predisposed him to love the arts, where he came to enjoy Provençal, a better instrument for poetry, back when the Italian language hadn't fully matured. So much did he love the combination of words with music, in which rhythm is a divine element, that throughout his life, despite asceticism and conflicts with others, poetry always sprang from his lips as a kind of mother's milk, lagging deep within the breast. His teachers should be thanked for this mark that makes a poet of the best of saints, putting a note of humanity into him, making him nearer to us.

Bernardone saw the danger of having an educated son. He is the classical, eternal type of father who breeds a tradesman or magistrate and who is, according to Richepin, suspicious of the delicate vice of literature.

So Bernardone interrupted his son's education so that he could devote his time to business. And he failed, in a classical, eternal type of failure: the boy stood behind the counter for some months, unwinding cloth, but one good day he left it all in disgust and became the partygoer whom we will see shortly.

Maybe the poet would have freed Bernardone from the later Saint, an outcome even worse for the stupid Bernardone than the young man with his quartettes. His mystic fatality collided with the ugliness of commerce and exacerbated the spiritual aspects of his nature. His second flight will go even further and he will betray more deeply the merchant's wishes. The tension will send the dart spinning up toward the sun.

La educación

En el matrimonio, a pesar de la benevolencia relativa del marido hacia la esposa, habrá siempre dos criterios distintos para juzgar las muchas cosas, el del plebeyo desaforado que ha hecho fortuna y manda, y el de la mujer dotada de alma mejor... En la educación de Francisco el choque fue visible. Pica quería hacer de su hijo joven letrado que completase la fundación del la casa en la que ya había ganancia suficiente; Pedro lo quiere por el contrario, continuador de sus viajes, entendido en contadurías con ojo de zorro para negocios escurridizos.

Pica sólo dijo su deseo, no luchó con el marido; era la esposa medieval y acababa por aceptar siempre.

Francisco empezó bajo la dirección de los religiosos de San Jorge su instrucción en letras. Fue discípulo estudioso y lleno de entusiasmo por el gran saber. Estaba hecho por su sensibilidad para el amor de las artes. De aquí le vendrá su gusto del provenzal, instrumento mejor para la poesía, en aquel tiempo en que el italiano no recibe aún su cuajadura. Tanto amaba la frase con música, en que el ritmo es elemento divino, que durante toda su vida, a pesar de ascetismos y batallas entre los hombres, siempre le vendrá a los labios el verso como una leche materna, rezagada en el fondo del pecho. Hay que agradecer a sus maestros esta huella que hará del mayor santo un poeta, poniéndole una nota de humanidad que lo hace como más próximo a nosotros.

Vio el Bernardone el peligro del hijo letrado. Él es el padre de todos los tiempos, engendrador de comerciante o magistrado, según Richepin, lleno de desconfianza hacia el vicio delicado de las letras.

Cortó, pues, Bernardone la educación de su hijo para dedicarlo al comercio. Y fracasó con el fracaso que también es de todos los tiempos; el niño estuvo algunos meses detrás de su mostrador desenvolviendo telas; pero un buen día dejó todo esto por repugnancia y se hizo el mozo de las fiestas que veremos luego.

Tal vez el poeta habría librado al necio Bernardone del Santo que vendría después y que había de ser más fatal para él que el joven de los serventesios. El choque del hombre fatalmente místico que había en el mozo con la fealdad del comercio, avivó, por exasperación, lo espiritual de su naturaleza. Su segundo vuelo irá muy lejos, y traicionará más todavía la voluntad del mercader; la tensión hará saltar el dardo a la altura del sol.

Francia, sept. 1926

LEPERS

Francis walked down the road to where the lepers lived, a road that had been as disgusting to him as to everyone because of the presence of filth that he could not forget, traveling along. Every time the young man in the velvet cap, the former Francis, faced the cursed house, he raised his cape to his eyes to avoid inhaling the stench that came with the wind. More than others, he was entitled to his disgust: he was young and beautiful, and youth is quick to get away from death and filth.

But at that very moment, like a bolt of lightning, words he had recently heard in the cave flashed across his mind.

"If you do what you fear, your fear will be exchanged for immense joy and great smoothness."

A leper was standing in the doorway, looking out at the road. Francis dismounts, walks directly up to him, and puts in the white, crumbling hand his abundant alms. Then he remained there, stock-still in front of him. Yes, the former Francis, the wastrel, could do only that, but the new one, who had been born again in the cave, had to go further. Yes, now he had to do more: he bowed and trembling, kissed the man's fingers. When he continued on his way, somewhat distracted, he felt as if a new freedom was making his body agile, and a huge softness, the invisible milk of charity, was bathing his heart.

But the next day he came along the same road, as before, like someone who has left a task half-done and is returning to finish it.

He enters the leper colony and when he arrives in their yard, the crowd of lepers, agitated by a stranger, surrounds him like a nightmare. They talk to him, showing their incomplete mouths and moving their arms as if to let their corruption breathe more freely. They draw close and touch him in their longing to feel something other than themselves, to feel solid flesh in someone else's arm. And there is Francis, standing stock-still among them as if his feet had suddenly taken root; living the tremendous minute of God, he is wide-eyed in surprise because all imagination has been overcome in the truly infinite, limitless illness. Illness enters through all of his senses: he sees, breathes, and touches it, and there is a moment when the stink makes him spin, as he feels faint. But he recovers, he steadies himself to continue looking, once again delivering his senses in order to complete the nameless test.

He pulls out his bag and begins to distribute his money. The greed of those who received it must have made the picture even more fantastic. There is nothing that his coins can do to repair those who almost don't have bodies. What delight will they feel in eating, when food only feeds the monster that spreads from head to feet, renewing the flesh as the gnawing of the poor living worm renews the mulberry leaf?

LA LEPRA

Francisco iba por el camino de la leprosería, camino que le había sido odioso como a todos por la presencia de la inmundicia que no podía olvidarse, pasando. Cada vez que el joven del birrete de terciopelo, el antiguo Francisco, enfrentaba la casa maldita, se subía la capa hasta los ojos para no aspirar la ola de fetidez que venía en el viento. Tenía más derechos que los otros a esta repugnancia: era joven y hermoso, y hay en la juventud el gesto rápido de apartar la muerte y la inmundicia.

Pero en el mismo momento, como un relámpago blanco, le alumbraron la mente las palabras recientes que había escuchado en la gruta.

"Si haces las cosas que hasta ahora te han espantado, se te trocarán en una inmensa alegría y una gran suavidad".

Un leproso estaba en la puerta, mirando hacia el camino. Francisco se desmonta, va derechamente hacia él y le pone en la mano desmoronada, que tiene la brasa blanca, su limosna abundante. Se quedó después parado delante de él. Si, el Francisco de ayer, de bolsa derramada, podía hacer solamente eso, pero el nuevo, que había nacido en la gruta por segunda vez, tenía que ir más allá. Sí, ahora había que hacer más, se dobló y temblando besó sus dedos. Siguió su camino, medio absorto, sentía que una libertad nueva hacia ágil su cuerpo y una suavidad inmensa, la leche invisible de la caridad le bañaba el corazón.

Pero al día siguiente vino por el mismo camino, como quien ha dejado una faena a medias y vuelve a acabarla.

Entra a la leprosería, y al llegar a su patio, la muchedumbre de los leprosos alborotada por un extraño, lo rodea como una pesadilla. Le hablan, haciendo más visibles sus bocas incompletas, mueven los brazos como para exhalar mejor su corrupción; se acercan, le tocan, por su ansia de palpar algo que no sea ellos mismos, de sentir en otro brazo la solidez de la carne; y allí está Francisco, en medio de ellos fijo como si sus pies en un momento hubiesen echado raíces viviendo el tremendo minuto de Dios, y con los ojos enormes de asombro porque toda imaginación ha sido superada en el mal ilimitado verdaderamente infinito. Entra el mal por todos sus sentidos, lo ve, lo aspira, lo toca, y hay un momento en que la fetidez lo hace volverse; porque siente un desmayo. Pero se recobra, se afirma para seguir mirando, entrega sus sentidos otra vez para acabar la prueba sin nombre.

Saca su bolsa y se pone a repartir su dinero. La avidez de los que recibían debió hacerle más fantástico el cuadro. Ninguna cosa allegan sus monedas a los que casi no tienen cuerpo. ¿Qué complacencia pondrán en sustentarse, si el alimento sólo alimenta el monstruo extendido de la cabeza a los pies, renovando la carne como renueva la hoja la morera por la roedura de la pobre viva?

The lepers move around him, constantly squabbling close to Francis. He continues distributing. But when he has finished, he looks at them and the frenzy that possesses him makes him continue. Now for the other alms: he will kiss each one on the mouth. They will have his mouth of a twenty-year-old like an unknown caress; they, who from the day when the first spot appeared, have received no kiss other than that of the blind and distant sun and who from utter pity have been washed by another, face averted . . .

The lepers, soothed by the abundant alms, sit down and look at him in utter astonishment. They look at him, beautiful, his limbs young and firm, and they see the human smile that they have almost forgotten, since they measure the illness, morning after morning, in the face of the nurse who hates them.

When he kissed the other one on the hand, the bones pretended to have some strength; this kiss differs from the larger one on the lips, in which the unspeakable softness of the worm is felt. And on kissing them too, a hotter, denser breath, as from an underground spring, comes out and bathes the face of the one who has, in an hour, gone crazy with mercy. Then he had to extinguish God's own pure world, his green Umbrian plain, and to disappear as if it had never existed. In the distance there is a leper who no longer has lips and who extends, to be kissed, dry gums and the arid whiteness of teeth.

The "invalids" probably thought that it was all a dream from the fever that never leaves them. But the dubious act stayed with them, as real as the coins in their hands.

Later on, various towns will enjoy the pleasure of his presence, but in over twenty years of ministry, of looking happily into that face, there was no one happier to have had him, not the monk León who loved him so much, or Pica, who put him to sleep at her breast. No one was happier than the filthy group at this supernatural hour.

Los leprosos se mueven sin dureza de contornos, se atropellan incesantemente alrededor de Francisco; él sigue repartiendo. Pero, cuando ha acabado, los mira y el frenesí que lo posee lo hace continuar. Ahora la otra limosna: él va a besar a cada uno la boca. Ellos tendrán su boca de veinte años como una caricia no conocida nunca, ellos, que desde el día en que se vieron la primera mancha, no han recibido sino el beso del sol que está ciego y distante y, por toda piedad, han sido lavados por otro con el rostro vuelto hacia atrás...

Los leprosos, aplacados por la limosna abundante, se han sentado y lo miran lleno de extrañeza. Lo miran hermoso, en sus miembros duros de juventud y le ven la sonrisa humana que casi han olvidado, porque ellos son esos que miden cada mañana el mal en la mueca del enfermero que los odia.

Cuando besó al otro en la mano, los huesos le fingían alguna firmeza; es otro este beso dado sobre los labios, grandes como un belfo, en que se siente la blandura indecible del gusano. Y al besar ellos también un aliento más caliente y más denso, como de fuente subterránea, sale de ellos y baña el semblante del que se ha vuelto en una hora loco de piedad. Entonces ha debido apagársele el mundo puro de Dios, su verde llanura Umbría, y desaparecer como si nunca hubiere existido. Más allá un leproso ya no tiene labios y pone para el beso la sequedad de la encía y el blanco árido de los dientes.

"Les malades" [los enfermos] pensaron seguramente que aquello era un sueño de la calentura que nunca los abandona. Pero del acto dudoso les quedaba como realidad las monedas en las manos.

Aunque más tarde un pueblo y otro pueblo gozarán de la presencia suya, en veinte años de apostolado felices de mirar ese semblante, ninguno de ellos, ni el fraile León que le amó tanto, ni Pica que lo durmió en su pecho, fueron más dichosos de haberlo tenido que el grupo inmundo de esta hora sobrenatural.

Francia, antes de oct. 1926

THE COMPANIONS OF ST. FRANCIS: BERNARD OF QUINTAVAL

The Rich Man

Bernard of Quintaval was young at the time of his conversion. In the Franciscan frescos, he has a beautiful face and an air of nobility.

He owned much land. Strong land endows its owner with a similar sense of powerful security. He had noble ancestry; that is, he easily found himself around men who paid attention to him. And with youth, he knew love, which possesses in the human face its greatest irradiation of power.

The Firstborn

Bernard became the first of the disciples, and thus the eldest in grace. This rapid joining covers him with nobility. He stands among those whose obedience to the call appears to have hastened the future, all brothers to John the Baptist.

In events at once human and divine, this birthright is celebrated above all else. Workers hastened by the Spirit possess it. They are the very opposite of Thomas, the man who, convinced of his touch, joins at the last minute. The ones who join early turn to saints long before miracles appear, like a fruit that can be felt all around. Hearing the visionary, they're as jolted as the others who saw a paralyzed man stand and walk.

Were they born with grace, so that their encounter was only a mutual recognition? Or is it that a life purer than other people's prepares them, as if with heart in hand, to submit? His "higher senses": was he born with them, while others were hard buds on whom love, the sun, must work further?

Whatever the case, on hearing the invitation, they stand up with an unearthly speed.

Conversion

Bernard of Quintaval was touched by the Saint's first preaching. That burning atmosphere of Franciscanism which subsequently makes for everyday conversions hadn't yet crystallized. More than this: the Pobrecito was still surrounded by the scandal of his city.

Bernard also doubted, but not for long. The storyteller says that Bernard de Quintaval, who was one of the city's "most prudent and noble rich men," began to see something wonderful in Francis: that disdain of the world causes shivering. But he grew doubtful, so he invited Francis to his house one night in order to be close to this beautiful field of auscultation. Bernard wasn't stingy

LOS COMPAÑEROS DE SAN FRANCISCO: BERNARDO DE QUINTAVAL

El hombre rico

Bernardo de Quintaval en el tiempo de la conversión era joven y en los frescos franciscanos tiene una bella fisonomía y un aire noble.

Poseía tierras, la tierra fuerte que pone en el dueño su misma seguridad poderosa; tenia abolengo, es decir, encontraba fácilmente a su alrededor la consideración de los hombres. Y con la juventud, era suyo el amor, que pone en el semblante humano la más grande irradiación de poder.

Los primogénitos

Vino a ser Bernardo el primero de los discípulos, el primogénito por lo tanto en la Gracia. Lo cubre la nobleza este acudir pronto, queda en el grupo de aquellos que para obedecer al llamado parecen que hubieran apresurado a la mañana; todos los hermanos de Juan Bautista.

En los sucesos ya humanos, ya divinos, esta primogenitura es celebrada por encima de las demás cosas. La poseen los obreros apresurados del Espíritu que son el tipo opuesto de Tomás, el convencido de su tacto, el hombre de última hora. Han acudido hacia los santos mucho antes de que ellos entregaran el milagro que, como un fruto, se puede palpar por todos sus costados; el sólo escuchar al iluminado les puso igual sacudida que a los otros cuando vieron que hacía al paralítico levantarse.

¿Habían nacido con la Gracia y el encuentro les fue solamente un reconocimiento? ¿O es que una vida más pura que la de los otros los tiene prontos, como si dijéramos con el corazón entre las manos para entregarlo? Sus "sentidos superiores", ¿les habían nacido ya mientras que en los otros eran yemas duras, en las cuales debe trabajar aún el sol, el amor?

Sea como sea, ello es, que se ponen de pie al escuchar la invitación, con una rapidez que no es de la tierra.

La conversión

Bernardo de Quintaval fue tocado por las primeras prédicas del Santo. Aún no se había cuajado esa atmósfera quemante del franciscanismo que hace después cotidianas las conversiones. Más que esto: todavía el pobrecito tenía en torno el escándalo de su ciudad.

También ha dudado Bernardo, pero no largamente... Dice el contador que Bernardo de Quintaval, que era de los "más nobles ricos y prudentes" de la ciudad, empezó a ver algo prodigioso en Francisco: aquel desdén del mundo que ponía

in taking precautions: he ordered a bed to be prepared for his guest in his own room, and he left a lighted lamp . . .

Francis understood none of this. He must have regarded Bernard's closeness as affection and the night light as a routine for going to sleep. He will also play with Bernard, hiding his true night from him, which had nothing to do with sleeping under meek eyelids.

Shortly after Bernard lay down, he began to snore loudly. The Pobrecillo saw him seemingly asleep and, knowing very little of mischief, arose to begin his long prayer, that prayer of his that made the night tremble like a veil.

He prayed with a painful contrition, with a real anguish that shook his chest like a cave at high tide; he prayed with much sorrow. He prayed for himself and "for the world that is wandering, lost." The images of his own life still drowned him, and he was harrowed prior to entering it, the time in whose violet flesh he would labor and groan for more than twenty years.

Half wrapped in sheets, Bernard was attending that prayer that was bathed in sweat like blood, and as he was looking at the suffering man, the spirit was at work within him. Although Francis's suffering tore at him, he didn't break that moment. By this point, it wasn't doubt that made him want more evidence. He was attending a secret ceremony in the depths of the night and he did not want to break the perfect moment.

But when Francis returned to his bed at dawn, Bernard said, "Brother, I am willing with all my heart to leave the world and to follow you wherever you may send me."

The storyteller says nothing of the wonder that St. Francis would have experienced when he realized he had been seen and on receiving such a weighty resolution from the "prudent man, noble and rich."

Only his answer is noted, as he advised Bernard that the seriousness of the case indicated that he should consult the Gospel.

They went off to a church and were praying until noon, and the answers given by the book, opened by the priest in three places, were these, as clear and insightful as three swords:

"If thou wilt be perfect, go and sell what you have, give to the poor and follow me."

"Take nothing for your journey, not a staff, scrip, sandals, or money."

"Whoever wishes to come after me must deny himself and take up his cross and follow me."

The words climb the scale. The first requires giving up goods; some people are capable of this. The second scales another immense rung; it involves not just giving, but uprooting the most innocent fleshly indulgences, of breathing and walking smoothly. A man could remain poor while keeping these things, which are a minimal concession for us.

calofrío. Pero dudaba, y para tener cerca esta preciosa materia de auscultación invitó a Francisco una noche a su casa. No fue avaro de precauciones puesto que hizo que se le preparara un lecho en su propia estancia y dejó encendida una lámpara...

Francisco no comprendía nada y debió tomar por afecto la proximidad de Bernardo y la luz por hábito nocturno. Él también va a jugar con Bernardo, a esconderle su verdadera noche que no era la del sueño bajo los párpados mansos.

Bernardo, a poco de acostarse, se puso a roncar ostensiblemente; el Pobrecillo lo miró dormido, sabía muy poco de malicias y se levantó para empezar su larga oración, aquella plegaria suya que hacía tremolar la noche como un velo.

Rezaba con una contrición penosa, con una angustia verdadera que agitaba su pecho como una gruta llena de alta marea; dolorosamente rezaba. Rogaba por él y "por el mundo que se perdía". Le ahogaban todavía las imágenes de su propia vida, y le atribulaba aún antes de entrar en ella, la época en cuya carne violeta iba a trabajar con gemidos más de veinte años.

Bernardo, medio envuelto entre sus sábanas, asistía a aquella plegaria bañada como de sudor de sangre y mirando al hombre sufriendo, el espíritu iba trabajando dentro de él. Aunque el sufrimiento de Francisco lo laceraba, él no rompió aquel momento. Ya no era la duda que le hiciese desear más pruebas; asistía a un acto secreto en el seno de la noche y no quería romper el instante perfecto.

Pero cuando Francisco volvió a su lecho al amanecer, Bernardo le dijo: "Hermano, yo estoy dispuesto de todo corazón a dejar el mundo y a seguirte en cuanto me mandares".

El contador no dice nada del asombro que se haría en San Francisco al comprender que había sido visto y al recibir tamaña resolución del "hombre prudente, noble y rico".

Anota solamente su respuesta, en la cual aconsejó a Bernardo que, por la gravedad del asunto, consultase el Evangelio.

Fueron hacia una Iglesia, se pusieron en oración hasta el mediodía y las respuestas que dio el libro abierto por el sacerdote en tres lugares, fueron estas claras y penetrantes como tres espadas:

"Si quisieres ser perfecto, ve y vende lo que tienes, dáselo a los pobres y sígueme".

"No lleves nada para el camino, ni bordón ni alforja ni sandalias ni dinero".

"El que quiera venir en pos de mí, niéguese a sí mismo, tome su cruz y sígame".

Las palabras que van en un ascendimiento. La primera obliga a la entrega de los bienes; de esto algunos son capaces; la segunda sube otro peldaño inmenso; no se trata sólo de dar, sino de arrancarse de las más inocentes complacencias corporales, la del aliento, la del suave caminar. Puede quedarse pobre el hombre, pero conservar estas cosas que son una mínima concesión a nosotros mismos.

The third sinks into heaven because denying oneself involves more than physical torment: there is the uprooting of whatever is in us that isn't Christ (and almost everything in us isn't Christ).

Division of Property

Bernard listened, unflinching. A true conversion, which is the complete inner reversal and tying of the innermost self, had already taken place within him. He left the church and went off to distribute his property.

Moving quickly also seems the mode of a superior nature, the rhythm that comes from another sphere. This man is going to hand over what belongs to him, as much as he has won by the toil of his own hands and as much as came into his hands from his elders, that is, possessions as beloved as beings nurtured with our blood, and possessions ennobled by our parents' having owned them.

A Superior Nature

A superior nature begins to work in him, which becomes a full light in the Spirit. Man has entered into the norm of the supernatural, and acts that are hard for us, which we perform waveringly on our plane, now sprout in that new state with the facility of the divine.

That was how Bernard was the first to "go naked." Days later, he experiences the feeling of his arms being full and his empty hands' greater weightlessness. He displays none of that deluded certainty that people will be dropping off a gift every fortnight. The rich man is suddenly taken up with a mouth worthy of the Gospel of renunciation. So did he come "to talk with God like one friend to another." There were none of the earthly cares that like heavy foliage come between us and the Lord, where we're caught up in our own voice. There was pure space between them, trembling.

St. Francis called him to talk about God and he went off to look for him in the jungle where Bernard was in ecstasy.

The minor monk didn't answer him. Francis continued to call him, and Bernard remained quiet. Francis called him a third time and as there was no answer, he became saddened by his companion's indifference. And in order to know the cause of that change, he began to pray and tell God about his sorrows. God the Father replied:

"Oh, poor little man! What has troubled you? Should a man leave God in order to answer the creature? Fray Bernard, as you were calling him, was with me and he could not answer, for he was beside himself."

Afterwards, full of shame, Francis asked, in a frenzy of humility, for one foot to be set on his neck and another over his mouth while saying words that would express contempt for his arrogance.

La tercera se hinca en el cielo, porque en el negarse a sí mismo hay más que el tormento corporal: hay la descuajadura de cuanto en nosotros no es Cristo (y lo que en nosotros no es Cristo es casi todo).

Reparto de los bienes

Bernardo escuchó sin vacilar; ya se había hecho dentro de él la volteadura de las entrañas que es la conversión verdadera; salió de la Iglesia y fue a repartir sus bienes.

El movimiento rápido parece también un modo de naturalidad superior, el ritmo de otra esfera. Este hombre va a entregar lo que le pertenece, cuanto ha ganado con los afanes propios y cuanto vino a sus manos desde sus mayores, es decir los bienes que se aman como a seres sustentados en nuestra sangre y los que están ennoblecidos por la posesión de nuestros padres.

Una naturalidad superior

Empieza en él una naturalidad superior hecha una luz plena en el espíritu; ha entrado el hombre en la norma sobrenatural y los actos duros que nosotros, en nuestro plano, hacemos jadeando, en aquel estado nuevo brotan con la facilidad que es lo divino.

Así es como Bernardo fue el primero en "acudir desnudo". El conoce en sí, en unos días, la sensación de los brazos colmados y de la mayor ingravidez en la mano vacía. No se ve en él ese camino largo de la convicción en el que otros van dejando caer cada diez jornadas un don; de un solo golpe el rico queda con la boca digna para el Evangelio de la renunciación. Por eso, llegó "a hablar con Dios como un amigo con otro", no había esa como fronda pesada que hacen los afanes de la tierra entre el Señor y nosotros, donde la propia voz se nos enreda. Quedó entre ellos el puro espacio tembloroso.

San Francisco lo llamaba para hablar de Dios con él y fue a buscarlo a la selva donde Bernardo estaba en éxtasis.

El fraile menor no le respondió. Volvió Francisco a llamarlo, y Bernardo siguió quieto; le llamó por tercera vez y no recibiendo respuesta se volvió triste por el desamor del compañero. Y para saber la causa de esa mudanza se puso a rezar y a contarle a Dios sus tristezas. El Padre le respondió:

"¡Oh pobre hombrecillo! ¿De qué te has turbado? ¿Debe el hombre dejar a Dios por la criatura? Fray Bernardo, cuanto tú le llamabas estaba conmigo, y no podía responder, pues se hallaba fuera de sí".

Después de este suceso fue cuando Francisco lleno de vergüenza le pidió, en un frenesí de humildad que pusiera un pie sobre su cuello y otro sobre su boca, diciéndole a la vez palabras que lo vilipendiaran de su soberbia.

Bernardo, antes de cumplir semejante mandato, que se le imponía, por la santa obediencia arrancó a Francisco la promesa de que él también le obedecería.

Before Bernard fulfilled the mandate imposed on him, by way of holy obedience he extracted from Francis a promise that he, too, would obey. What he asked, then, was that Francis would correct him harshly whenever they were together.

So did the two "fools of God" exchange vows of obedience, and they vowed to wash one another as they washed the lepers. They were as clear as two crystals, each crossing the other with their light.

Preaching in Bologna

Bernard, commanded by Francis, goes to Bologna where the barbaric scene of Assisi is repeated. The poor figure that Bernard presented there, in his old clothes and maybe even his very air of complete absorption, unleashed on him the brutality of the mob.

A crowd followed him, shouting. To placate the horde with his patience, he sat in the middle of the town square. The children jostled his hood and his sleeves, and the men threw stones . . . Bernard, "without changing his posture," looked at them calmly. They would have to get tired and then they would listen to him.

And this lasted until a man who had studied law at the university, who was well regarded in the city, wanted to put him under his protection.

"Who are you? Why you come here?" he asked.

Fray Bernard's only answer was to slide his hand onto his chest, and he pulled out the rule of St. Francis and gave it to him to read.

What the Doctor would say to the people of Bologna about Franciscanism are timeless words:

"Truly I have never heard of a higher state of religion than this."

Immediately he offers the monk his house for a monastery, and he becomes their advocate in the city. From the very moment that the lawyer spoke in such ascendant terms, the townspeople begin coming to hear the preacher. They pour so much praise on him that he feels forced to leave. When he returns, he tells the saint that he has come because of the many honors that he received there in the city, "fearing to lose more than he gained with them."

Temptations

Francis had received a message that Bernard would be engaging in many battles with the devil; for that reason, he especially prayed for him.

For the masses (including educated people with uncouth minds), the temptations of the saints are always fighting with nakedness that pulsates over the desert. But the most difficult temptations of the mystics have been something else entirely. They are the dry periods of which St. [Teresa of Avila] speaks; the

Lo que pidió después fue que Francisco le corrigiese ásperamente cada vez que estuviesen juntos.

Así cambiaban votos de obediencia los dos embriagados de Dios y se juraban lavarse mutuamente, como se lavan los leprosos, ellos que eran claros como dos cristales y que se atravesaban uno a otro con sus destellos.

Prédica de Bolonia

Bernardo, mandado por Francisco, va a Bolonia donde se repite la escena bárbara de Asís. La pobre figura en que ha parado Bernardo, sus ropas viejas, y tal vez hasta su mismo aire absorto, desencadenaron sobre él la brutalidad de la plebe.

Una poblada le seguía entre gritos, él para aplacarla con su paciencia, se sentó en medio de la plaza. Los niños lo zarandeaban por la capucha y las mangas, y los hombres le tiraban piedras... Bernardo, "sin mudar la postura", los miraba tranquilamente. Habían de cansarse y después lo escucharían.

Y esto duró hasta que un licenciado, lleno de consideración en la ciudad, quiso cubrirlo con su amparo.

"¿Quién eres tú y por qué has venido aquí?" preguntó.

Fray Bernardo, por toda contestación, metió la mano en su pecho y sacó la regla de San Francisco y se la dio para que la leyese.

Lo que el Doctor dirá a las gentes de Bolonia sobre el franciscanismo son palabras eternas:

"Verdaderamente éste es el más alto estado de religión que yo he oído nunca".

En seguida ofrece al fraile menor casa para un convento y se hace su defensor en la ciudad. Desde que el licenciado habló ascendientemente, la población va aproximándose a escuchar al predicador; llegan a colmarlo de tantas alabanzas que lo hacen salir de ella. A su vuelta dice al Santo que se ha venido por los muchos honores recibidos en ella, "temiendo perder más de lo que ganaba con ellos".

Tentaciones

Francisco había recibido mensaje de que Bernardo debería sostener muchas batallas con el demonio; de aquí que rezaba por él especialmente.

Para el vulgo (léase también los cultos de mente grosera), las tentaciones de los santos son siempre combates con desnudeces que laten sobre el desierto. Pero las tentaciones más duras de los místicos han sido otras. Son las sequedades de que habla la Santa, el mudárseles de pronto la humedad del corazón en limaduras de yesca y hacerles entonces una oración áspera como el polvo de la yesca también; son las caídas peores en la materia, la desesperación de no

sudden transformation in the heart's moisture becomes dry, crumbling tinder, making prayer as harsh as sawdust. They are the worst descents into the material world, the despair of not reaching Grace, anguish like the one whose cry is returned by the caves.

Tremendous mystery of the inner life. This has, like the earth, happy areas and blankets of dried lava. The intensity of the mystic's inner life sometimes seems to burn the soul.

Other temptations, savoring of sexuality, are less serious. Their outlines are highlighted by color and are distinctly visible.

Those temptations are scarcely recognizable; only the mystic's eye, knowing about crystals, can make them out like breath that fogs over a glass.

alcanzar la Gracia; una angustia como la de aquel cuyo grito es devuelto por las grutas.

Tremendo misterio de la vida interior. Esta tiene, como la tierra, zonas dichosas y mantos de lava seca. De intensa, la vida interior del místico, parece que en algunos momentos quema el alma.

Las demás tentaciones, saboreo de lúbricos, son menos graves; tienen coloreado el contorno y su relieve es visible.

Aquellas apenas se las reconoce; sólo el ojo del místico, sabio en cristales, puede advertirlas como la empañadura de un aliento...

Francia, antes de oct. 1926

PRAYER

How did St. Francis pray? Would he let the Friend's confidences flow like a spring and whisper in wordless conversation in the crests of the soul?

If St. Theresa has given us, as an image of prayer, the deep water wheel from which the overflowing buckets arise, you merely gave us the example of your prayer as a litany in the rhythm of the heart in love:

"My Lord and my God," you were saying, linking the prayer with the breathing of all the creatures who sleep trusting in our Father who never sleeps,

"My Lord and my God" in diastole and systole, through the auricle of the Italian night, wounded by the cypresses as is Israel by Caesar's lances.

"My Lord and my God" in the same rhythm as the sap from the olive trees that bow down with accumulated oil, anointing even their roots.

"My Lord and my God" as women give birth and pain becomes joy for them, hearing the newborn's cry, which veins the Carrara marble.

"My Lord and my God" becomes increasingly smooth and serene as the old man who is dying, at whose headboard you and his guardian angel watch and assist.

"My Lord and my God" as the stanza, laden with the well's silence, pours into the poet, cut by a shooting star that slips into a mouth on the verge of complaining.

"My Lord and my God" to the unison of all the seas' waves tossing their brine like the adulterous man admitting his guilt to his partner.

Just like Christ, St. Francis went off to pray, far from men, as he hungered for silence and thirsted for solitude. He had a passion for obedience and wanted to constrain his will and not "lean unto his own understanding," just like the martyr waterfall when it lets itself collapse into the arms of the one who turns it into a foamy cloud and who then raises it up by way of the rainbow.

Protected by a chapel of bushes at the mountain's summit as Brother León and St. Rufino watched over the community, at last St. Francis could forget the doors that didn't lock, that any brother could open, peeking in, seeking help. He could also ignore the bell that some gentleman rocked back and forth as he sought counseling for his soul.

Others would help in your name. Others would settle the disputes brought to the monastery, for many became Franciscans from your example day in, day out, and throughout the day.

You could well pass the staff onto others to manage, leaving it to the divine shepherd. A brave but fragile sheep licking the neck of the good shepherd that carries her: "My Lord and my God. My Lord and my God."

LA ORACIÓN

¿Cómo rezaría San Francisco? ¿Dejaría que la confidencia del Amigo manase como un venero y le fuera susurrando la conversación sin palabras en las cimeras del alma?

Si Santa Teresa nos ha dado por imagen de la oración, la profunda noria, de la cual se hacen subir los cántaros colmados, tú, sólo nos diste el ejemplo de tu oración vuelta letanía al compás del corazón enamorado:

"Señor mío y Dios mío", decías, enlazando a la plegaria el respiro de todas las criaturas que duermen fiadas a nuestro Padre que jamás duerme.

"Señor mío y Dios mío" en diástole y sístole, a través de la aurícula de la noche italiana, herida por los cipreses como Israel por las lanzas de César.

"Señor mío y Dios mío" al mismo ritmo que la savia de los olivos que se doblan de óleo acumulado y ya ungen sus raíces.

"Señor mío y Dios mío" mientras las mujeres dan a luz y el dolor se les vuelve gozo al escuchar el vagido, que vetea los mármoles de Carrara.

"Señor mío y Dios mío" mientras aceza cada vez más suave y sereno el anciano que se está muriendo y a cuya cabecera lo ayudas con su Ángel custodio.

"Señor mío y Dios mío" en tanto que al poeta le mana la estrofa agravada por el silencio del pozo y cortada por un aerolito que le cae a la boca cuando va a quejarse.

"Señor mío y Dios mío" al unísono de las olas de todos los mares que están volteando su salmuera como el adúltero que se denuncia ante su compañera.

Igual que Cristo, igual, se retiraba San Francisco a orar lejos de los hombres, porque tenía hambre de silencio, sed de soledad, pasión de obediencia y quería amarrar la voluntad y deponer el entendimiento, igual que la cascada mártir que se deja caer en brazos de quien la hace nube de espuma y luego la alza a través del arco iris.

Tutelado por una capilla de matorrales en el ápice de un monte, mientras Fray León y San Rufino celaban la comunidad, al fin podía San Francisco olvidarse de puertas sin cerrojo, que cualquier hermano entreabría buscando ayuda; y desentenderse también de campana remecida por algún caballero que solicitaba consejo para su alma.

Otros darían auxilio en su nombre, otros resolverían los agravios que eran llevados al convento, pues eran muchos los que habían sido afranciscanados por su ejemplo de cada día y de tantas veces al día.

Bien podía pasar el báculo a otros mayorales, y dejarse pastorear a lo divino. Oveja frágil pero valiente, lamiendo el cuello del Buen Pastor que la acarrea: "Señor mío y Dios mío. Señor mío y Dios mío".

Provenza, Francia, 1927

OUR ONLY PRIDE

St. Paul defined charity as "the most emphatic demonstration of love." Lacking it, measuring it, the most evident holiness is reduced to mere noise without affection: cacophony of brass, a wooden bell . . . the fall of that giant that Daniel saw, tall as a shining lighthouse, plated in silver and gold, whose clay feet could not support that cold, weighty splendor.

Francis, with this architectural gift that appears in mystics and poets, lifts up his happiness chair by chair until constructing for us the campanile of perfect joy. It tells us that a monk may achieve the most prodigious wonders and know the unfathomable and even speak in the tongue of angels, yet can, even so, lack perfect joy.

And Francis keeps accumulating that monk's wonders, lifting them upwards in a stairway of perfections . . . we who are imperfect remain troubled: what, then, is *perfect joy?*

"A mystery of free will," you answer. With your clear and transparent words you say that these robes and crowns that divine love gives lovingly to the soul in love are gifts, precious things, donations from God to man. But what is uniquely ours, owned in full possession, is the cross that we accept, our own: the only pride that we deserve. And in bearing it, as welcome and fully ours as our own soul, perfect joy bursts forth like the good smoke that wafted up from Abel's praise. That joy, Francis, enabled you to welcome whatever would make nails more like nails, and the cross more of a cross.

NUESTRA ÚNICA VANAGLORIA

San Pablo definió la caridad como "la más rotunda demostración del amor". Faltando ella, raleando ella, las santidades más ostensibles se reducen a mera resonancia sin cariño: algarabía de bronces, campana de palo... La falla de aquel gigantón que viera Daniel, alto como un faro reluciente, enchapado en plata y oro, pero cuyos pies de barro no pudieron sostener ese esplendor pesado y frío.

Francisco, con ese don arquitectónico que se da en místicos y poetas, alza su bienaventuranza sillar por sillar hasta labrarnos el campanil de la alegría perfecta. Nos aclara que aunque un fraile logre las maravillas más portentosas, conozca lo insondable e incluso hable en lengua de ángeles, aún así carece de la alegría perfecta.

Y Francisco sigue acumulando los prodigios de ese fraile, los alza en una escalera de perfecciones... imperfectas, que nos dejan conturbados: ¿cuál es, entonces, *la alegría perfecta*?

Respondes un misterio de albedrío. Dices con tus palabras transparentes, que esos ropajes y coronas que el amor divino entrega enamoradamente al alma enamorada, son regalos, preseas, donaciones de Dios al hombre. Pero que lo único nuestro, cabalmente nuestro, poseído con total posesión, es la cruz que aceptamos, la propia: única vanagloria que merecemos. Y del llevarla tan bienvenida y tan nuestra como el alma, prorrumpe la alegría perfecta, como se izaba el humo certero de la alabanza de Abel. Esa alegría, Francisco, te hizo capaz de acoger a cuanto hiciese más clavos los clavos, y más cruz la cruz.

Provenza, Francia, 1927

SURRENDER (FIRST VERSION)

You would have liked to immerse yourself in the godmotherly silence that nurtures its mosses and springs like a good cave. Leave the city; get away from the bustle of the town squares where Italian ferocity suddenly flares with the bravado that Shakespeare portrays in *Romeo and Juliet* . . . And where you, Francis, took part, better than Romeo between Tybalt and Mercutio, even separating the hotheaded boys, fierce as wild boars, turning them into a couple of dogs sniffing each other in friendship. But your retreat had been torn like the shirts of these vehement creatures . . . Then you retired into the quiet of the nearest chapel. There, with much patience and great care, as if it were your robe, you patched tranquility; you mended the peace so that you could continue talking to your Friend.

Other times, the monks came to your cell with domestic mishaps that they regarded as vast as a tower's collapse, when it was nothing but a sack of wheat that spilled over the kitchen floor. Shattered from your *convivio,* your banquet, you return to it in the cave of your cell or in the cloud of a bush. (Artists also wanted to make a cell of their workshops, to strengthen their work there, and even disappear like an almond in its shell.)

Having become a father to so many children, you could not be like hermits and fully give yourself over to meditation. Still, you would have liked to have a little more quiet nearby, a few longer, more protected hours to be with Christ. That was why the donation that Maese Orlando made to you of a hill in Tuscany filled you with delight. A mountain well-supplied with forests and stones for sheltering prayer. Maese Orlando described it to you without enthusiasm. You already saw how that stony grove invited mortification and prayer. In that wild basilica, opening his wounds in your body, Christ had chosen to make you a brother in his Passion. But before climbing your Mount Tabor, you wondered what you should do. Pray in total surrender to God? Found across Italy and France a myriad of monasteries, scattered like oases across the Sahara? Stay alone with your Friend or bring more friends to your Friend? Burn in solitude in His secret word? Or go out with that word, setting the world afire?

You consulted Christ, then, by way of your brothers and Clare. They all answered with the same words that the Good Shepherd wanted you to expand his flock.

Against your chest, something insisted, something wounded, like those tumbleweeds that the wind begins to roll across the plains until they crash into the walls of a city. As with Benedict, God wanted to sanctify you by

LA ENTREGA
(PRIMERA VERSIÓN)

Tú hubieras querido sumergirte en el silencio que amadrina, como la buena gruta, sus musgos y fuentes. Ponerte lejos de la ciudad, distanciarte de la algarabía de las plazas donde la fiereza italiana se encendía con esas bravatas súbitas que Shakespeare retrata en "Romeo y Julieta". Y donde tú, Francisco, intervenías, mejor que Romeo entre Teobaldo y Mercucio, hasta separar los muchachos enardecidos, fieros como jabalíes, volviéndolos un par de perros que se olfatean amigados. Pero ya tu recogimiento había sido rasgado como las camisas de esos vehementes... Entonces te retirabas al sosiego de la capillita más próxima y ahí, con mucha paciencia, con gran esmero como si fueran tu sayal, remendabas el sosiego, zurcías la paz, hasta poder seguir hablando con tu Amigo.

Otras veces, a tu celda acudían los frailes con un percance doméstico, que a ellos les parecía colosal como el colapso de una torre, y que no pasaba de ser la caída de un saco de trigo sobre las baldosas de la cocina. Desquiciado de tu convivio, de nuevo te abocabas a recuperarlo en la gruta de tu celda o en la nube de un matorral. (También el artista querría hacer de su taller una celda y allí afianzar su obra, hasta desaparecer en ella como la almendra en su nuez).

Vuelto padre de tantos hijos, no podías, como los ermitaños, cederte por entero a la meditación, pero hubieras querido un poquito más de tranquilidad en torno, unas horas más largas y protegidas para estar con Cristo. Por eso te llenó de alegría la donación que te hiciera maese Orlando, de un monte en la Toscana. Un monte bien dispuesto con bosques y piedras para cobijar la oración. Te lo describía sin entusiasmo maese Orlando, y ya ibas viendo cómo esa arboleda pedregosa convidaba a mortificarse y rezar. En esa basílica silvestre, abriendo sus llagas en tu cuerpo, había escogido Cristo hermanarte a su Pasión. Pero antes de subir a tu monte Tabor, te preguntaste qué debías hacer: ¿la oración en la total entrega a Dios, o la fundación, en Italia y Francia, de una pléyade de conventos, espaciados como los oasis del Sahara? ¿Quedarte solo con tu Amigo o llevarle más amigos a tu Amigo? ¿Arder solitario en su palabra secreta o salir a incendiar con ella el mundo?

Consultaste entonces a Cristo, mediante tus hermanos y Clara; todos respondieron, con las mismas palabras, que el Buen Pastor quería contigo magnificar su grey.

Contra tu pecho algo porfiaba, algo hería, como esas bolas de cardos sueltos que el viento echa a rodar por las planicies hasta que se estrellan contra las murallas de una ciudad. A la manera de Benito, Dios te quería santificar mediante

creating an Order with a rule and monasteries for the rule. Sent out to get you to say "Amen," that legion of thistles drubbed at your conscience, and bruising you, didn't leave you alone. Until you felt ashamed at being so stone blind on top of being so stone deaf, and the call had to add thorns in order to spur you on.

la creación de una Orden, con regla, y conventos para la regla. Enviada a sacarte el amén, esa legión de cardos tundía tu conciencia, y magullándote, no te dejaba tranquilo. Hasta que sentiste vergüenza de ser tan piedra ciega encima de tanta piedra sorda, y que el llamado tuviese que ponerse púas para espolearte.

Provenza, Francia, 1927

SURRENDER, THE CALL OF THE THISTLES (SECOND VERSION)

In the midst of the city, in the hubbub of the markets, Italian ferocity, ready to flare up like dry grass, caught fire in that sudden bravado that Shakespeare stokes in his *Romeo and Juliet.* You, Francis, took part better than Mercutio and managed, without hurting yourself, to separate the scorpions and turn them into a couple of affectionate dogs. But your seclusion was torn like the white shirts of those madmen. In order to mend your calm in the stillness of the nearest chapel, you would have had to retreat and there, very patiently, you would wait, hoping that your Friend would want to continue talking to you. And if not, you would speak like one who accompanies a prisoner.

Friars would sometimes come to your cell with a domestic accident that struck them as being as colossal as the collapse of a tower, but which was no more than a sack of flour that fell and spilled onto the pantry tiles.

Once again, they had shattered your "convivio." Once again, you recovered in the calm of your cell or behind a bush. Being the spiritual father of so many children, you knew that it wasn't possible for you to give yourself over to endless meditation like anchorites and hermits. You understood that the shepherd can't forget his shelter. But you wished that there was a little more calm around you to spur on your communication with Christ and enter into the silence as in a self-enclosed cave.

One good day all your distress gathered, spread, and reached your chest, like those tumbleweeds that the wind begins rolling along the plains and that strike the city walls until they disintegrate into stray thorns. What was pricking your heart was the restlessness of the mystic who feels bifurcated in quiet stone with moss, and in rolling without any moss, is simultaneously called by the two ways to love Christ: of Martha or Mary; one stationary, the other busy. You felt the call of the Heroic One, for it had to do with deeds, and what deeds! To go off preaching, no less, and to found a network of monasteries across Italy and France, scattered like wells across the Sahara.

You consulted Christ by way of your brothers and Clare. Choosing the same words, they told you that you should expand the pastorate that the Good Shepherd required of his apprentice.

Like Benedict, you would be sanctified through the creation of an Order with a rule and monasteries. And to hurry you, the thistles called against your chest.

LA ENTREGA, LA LLAMADA DE LOS CARDOS (SEGUNDA VERSIÓN)

En medio de la ciudad, en la algarabía de los mercados, la fiereza italiana, pronta a llamear como los pastos secos, se incendiaba en esas súbitas bravatas que Shakespeare atiza en su "Romeo y Julieta". Tú, Francisco, intervenías, mejor que Mercucio, y lograbas, sin herirte, separar a los alacranes y luego volverlos un par de perros querendones. Pero tu recogimiento había quedado rasgado como las blancas camisas de aquellos energúmenos. Tendrías que retirarte a zurcir tu sosiego dentro del sosiego de la capillita más próxima y ahí, con mucha paciencia, esperar a que tu Amigo quisiera seguir hablando contigo. Y si no quería, hablarle tú como quien acompaña a un encarcelado.

También a veces, a tu celda acudían los frailes con un percance doméstico que a ellos les parecía colosal como el colapso de una torre, y que no pasaba de ser la caída de un saco de harina derramado sobre las baldosas de la despensa.

De nuevo te habían desquiciado del convivio y otra vez te recuperarías en el sosiego de tu celda o dentro de un matorral. Sabías que siendo padre espiritual de tantos hijos, no era posible que te cedieras a la incesante meditación, de los anacoretas y ermitaños. Entendías que el pastor no puede olvidar su aprisco. Pero hubieras deseado un poquito más de tranquilidad en torno, para celar tu comunicación con Cristo y poder entrar en el silencio como en una gruta ensimismada.

Un buen día toda tu desazón se acumuló, cundió y alcanzó a tu pecho, como esas bolas de cardos que el viento echa a rodar por las planicies y que golpean las murallas de una ciudad hasta que se desmenuzan en un reguerillo de púas. Eso que te estaba punzando el corazón era la inquietud del místico que se siente bifurcado en quieta piedra con musgo, y en rodado sin musgo alguno, llamado a la vez por los dos modos de amar a Cristo: el de Marta o el de María; el uno inmóvil, el otro ajetreando. Sentías la llamada del Hazañoso, porque de hazaña ¡y de cuánta hazaña! se trataba: nada menos que ir a predicar y fundar en Italia y en Francia, una red de conventos, distribuidos como las cisternas del Sahara.

Consultaste a Cristo mediante tus hermanos y Clara; escogiendo las mismas palabras te dijeron que debías magnificar el pastoreo que el Buen Pastor requería de su aprendiz.

A la manera de Benito, te santificarías mediante la creación de una Orden, con regla y conventos. Y para apresurarte los cardos llamaban contra tu pecho.

Provenza, Francia, 1927

ANOTHER CHRIST

The sins of this earth smelled so bad that God the Father wanted to raise his hand and bring the stubborn ones to justice. The Son, taking pity, promised to renew his life and passion into a creature that would be a new offering from the Son to the Father, a dove next to the lamb, gift of God to God, by way of a man. For that Francis was born in Italy, where passions and cypresses pierce the sky, so that in him we would have a *brother* in Christ, his standard bearer, with twelve monks for the twelve apostles, an Italian Christ, mirror of the Nazarene.

But humanity was so maggoty in this tremendous thirteenth century that the Virgin, in the same impulse toward mercy as her Son, wanted to renew all her virginal purity and humility in another woman. She appealed, then, to the love of Sister Clare, Virgin of Assisi: a mirror of the Immaculate of Nazareth, who tore thousands of women from the claws of the devil.

If the soul of Francis was Christ, the body wasn't, not yet. He hadn't yet been given the genuine wounds of His Passion. And opening them in the flesh with nails of iron, as decided and resounding as those that bar the gates of Sienna and emerge on the other side, black and shiny as beetles of Egypt. Nails that must work until the trumpets of the Final Judgment sound and open all doors, and the whole universe bursts wide open so that all those crucified with love may go forth, bearing the marks of His blood. Nails as heavy as the hilts of swords and that when you go barefoot, moaning in the privacy of your cell, they resound with a metallic clang that made the devil cringe, where he was painted on the walls. Nails of the fourth cross, which only María could see: the nails of Francis on Golgotha, alongside the nails of Assisi.

With what modesty did you hide your well-wounded feet, wrapped in wool and set into sandals where the nails remain as secret as the seed in the *lúcuma* fruit? And walking, you scarcely left a contented blow of bruised fruit.

Knocking on the portals of glory, they put nails in your reddened palms. Mercy will open them as they await the call at the door.

You close your sleeves as the rose closes its petals to hide the stamens. Now you use just one to hand to confer blessings, with the haste of a traveling Bishop. Brother Leo and your brothers, always aware of your slightest gestures, are struck by this oddity. The farmers, who had previously seen you drawing a sign of the cross in the air, tenderly and lingering in tenderness, began to think that you weren't putting all of the blessing in the hand and that its grace wafted in on the wind.

You ate even less and you drank the glass of water, raising it to your mouth with the slowness of the Eucharistic chalice. The slightest friction hurt you,

OTRO CRISTO

Tanto hedían los pecados de esta Tierra, que Dios Padre quiso alzar su mano y ajusticiar a los contumaces. El Hijo, apiadándose, prometió renovar su vida y pasión en una criatura que fuese ofrenda nueva del Hijo al Padre, paloma junto al cordero, dádiva de Dios a Dios, vía un hombre. Para eso fue engendrado Francisco en Italia, donde las pasiones y los cipreses punzan el cielo: para que en él tuviésemos un *hermano* de Cristo, portaestandarte y confaloniero suyo, con doce frailes por doce apóstoles, un Cristo Italiano, espejo del Nazareno.

Pero tan agusanada estaba la humanidad en ese tremendo siglo XIII, que quiso la Virgen, al mismo ímpetu de misericordia que su Hijo, renovar en otra mujer toda su pureza y humildad virginales. Recurrió entonces al amor de sor Clara, Virgen de Asís: espejo de la Purísima de Nazaret, quien arrancó de zarpas del demonio a millares de mujeres.

Si el alma de Francisco era Cristo, el cuerpo todavía no. Faltaba darle las genuinas llagas de Su Pasión. Y abrírselas en la carne con clavos de hierro, indudables y rotundos como esos que traspasan los portones de Siena y afloran al otro lado, negros y relucientes como los escarabajos de Egipto. Clavos que han de servir hasta que suenen las trompetas del juicio Final y se abran todas las puertas, y el universo entero esté de par en par, para que todos los crucificados de amor vayan llegando por las huellas de Su sangre. Clavos que pesan como pomos de espadas y que cuando ibas descalzo, gimiendo en la intimidad de tu celda, daban un campaneo metálico que hacía encarrujarse al demonio untado en los muros. Clavos en cuyo destellar de obsidiana, tú contemplabas la súbita noche de Jerusalén, enlutada por su Rey. Clavos de la cuarta cruz, que sólo María pudo ver: los clavos de Francisco de Gólgota, junto a los clavos de Asís.

Con qué pudor escondías tus pies bienheridos, forrándolos en lanas y metiéndolos en sandalias donde los clavos quedaban secretos como el semillón en la lúcuma. Y al caminar dabas apenas un ledo golpeteo de frutas magulladas.

Bulto de aldabones de la gloria, ponían los clavos en tus palmas enrojecidas, ante las cuales se abrirá misericordia que está aguardando a que le den de aldabonazos.

Cerrabas las mangas, como la rosa que aprieta sus pétalos por esconder los estambres. Bendecías ahora con una como premura de obispo en viaje, que extraño a Fray León y a tus hermanos, atentos siempre a tus gestos más leves. Los campesinos que antes te habían visto dibujar en el aire, una gran señal de la cruz, tiernamente y demorándote en la ternura, pensaron que ahora no ponías toda la bendición en la mano y que su ola de gracia venía ladeada por el viento.

Comías aún menos y bebías el vaso de agua subiéndolo a la boca con la lentitud del cáliz eucarístico. Cualquier roce te dolía, como al quemado, y se

like one who has been burned, and your lips grew weary of repressing groans. The monks believed that you drank with a priestly gesture, always raising the vessel as if it held blood; and so it did, but offering the blood of your wounds to Christ.

Alone in your cell, you felt a trickle of blood rolling from torso to hip, you stuck your shirt on the boil, so that the canvas would drink up what was spilled. Brother Leon, who was responsible for washing your clothes, saw these red dahlias in the cloth, knowing and not knowing whom he served.

Jesus Christ, in a kind of seraph, let you feel some of his pain and go down to Limbo just as he did to bring up your brothers and followers. You wanted them to know it. But Christ had not commanded you to share joy or keep a secret. What to do?

An Illuminated Brother answered your concerns: "If you're hiding what God wanted to give you for the benefit of many, you deserve rebuke."

Yours had been a fire of love and all of Mount Varnia was sounding the alarm to shepherds and travelers. What could be seen from afar in a kind of fire must later be seen turned into sores, clearly and from a hand's span of distance, when the new Thomas, now called Jerome, touched in order to believe. Second cloth of Veronica, flag of Christ!

Francis, once you lay dead, your hands folded like a dove on your chest and your feet like two fish stranded upon your shroud, the citizens of Assisi came to verify your wounds. And that Jerome who so boldly touched your nails one by one, who measured with his index finger the slit on the side, as big as a laurel leaf, had to become their minister and swear on the Bible every time someone doubted as he had doubted.

Thanks to believing in you, Francis, your ardent love convinced me without any need of seeing these emblems turning red in your body.

fatigaban tus labios de retener los quejidos. Creían los frailes que bebías con gesto sacerdotal, que siempre alza el vaso como si llevara sangre; así era, pero ofreciendo a Cristo la sangre de tus llagas.

Cuando a solas en tu celda, sentiste un reguero de sangre rodar del torso a la cadera, apegaste la camisa sobre la llaga, para que el lienzo se bebiese la derramadura. Fray León encargado de lavar tu ropa, vio esas dalias rojas en la tela, pero no preguntó nada, sabiendo y no sabiendo a quién servía.

Jesucristo, en especie de serafín, te había otorgado sentir algo de sus dolores y bajar como Él al Limbo para sacar de allí hermanos y seguidores tuyos. Tú querías que lo supieran. Pero Cristo no te había mandado compartir gozo ni guardar secreto. ¿Qué hacer?

A tu inquietud contestó Fray Iluminado: "Si oculto tienes lo que Dios te ha querido dar para utilidad de muchos, merecedor seas de reprensión".

Lo tuyo había sido un incendio de amor y todo el monte Varnia llameaba alertando a pastores y viajeros. Lo que de lejos se divisaba en especie de fuego, habría de verse después vuelto llagas, con toda claridad y a sólo un palmo de distancia, cuando el nuevo Tomás, ahora llamado Jerónimo, palpara hasta creer. ¡Segundo paño de la Verónica, bandera de Cristo!

Francisco, cuando ya reposabas muerto, con las manos en paloma sobre el pecho y los pies en dos peces varados sobre tu mortaja, acudieron los ciudadanos de Asís a comprobar tus llagas. Y ese Jerónimo que tan osadamente tocó tus clavos uno por uno, y que midió con su índice la hendidura del costado, grande como una hoja de laurel, tuvo que volverse ministro de ellas y jurar sobre la Biblia cada vez que alguien dudaba como él había dudado.

Gracias por creer en ti, Francisco, sin tener que ver esos emblemas rojeando en tu cuerpo: con tu ardiente caridad me convenciste.

Provenza, Francia, 1927

THE WOLF IN HEAVEN

A man as slow and weak as a lamb in a year of drought walked toward me, leaving riotous men behind.

His eyes on mine: I felt that all my savagery was swallowed and returned as streams of love. Within that whole look, his heart beat so softly that it calmed the rough beating of my wolfish heart.

On asking me in human fashion to take his paw, in his warm palm's touch I felt the same wellspring as in his gaze. A hand from which to drink as much of the best that a body could offer, a hand for sniffing and licking until becoming brothers, a hand that could gather coals without being burned and could bend horseshoes without its veins swelling. He blessed me with such a hand and I felt his tenderness filling my body.

Now I know what is to be blessed and go through the forest as a newborn, to sleep as boldly as the mountains at night, and to awake with birdsong, giving thanks at finding myself again in the light.

The Agubbios behaved well and kept their promise like good wolves, feeding me, as agreed. So have I aged between the forest and the walled city, coming and going from the dense forests of beech trees to the high towers, and from the winding streets to the narrow ravines. But every night I would come to sleep in the open spaces where I met the human lamb here, next to the stone where he gave me his hand and blessed my heart.

With my old muscles growing stiff and with these tired eyes that could no longer distinguish your silhouette, I awaited your return, Francis. I faced morning after morning for you until I realized that we would never see each other again in these places, divided between forests and cities. Then I went off to lie on the grass of our first meeting and let myself grow cold under the stars.

The people of Agubbio found me silver with frost, and when I saw them pick me up lovingly and take me to church, I barked a thunderclap at them before running toward the stars.

EL LOBO EN EL CIELO

Un hombrecito lento y flaco como cordero en año de sequía, caminaba hacia mí, dejando atrás a los hombres alborotados.

Sus ojos puestos en mis ojos: sentí que toda mi fiereza era sorbida por ellos y luego devuelta a raudales de cariño, y que entero en esa mirada, su corazón latía tan suavemente que serenaba los bruscos latidos de mi corazón de lobo.

Al pedirme, según la usanza de los hombres, que le tendiese una zarpa, toqué sobre su palma tibia el mismo venero de la mirada. Mano para beber en ella cuanto un cuerpo puede dar de óptimo, mano para olfatearla y lamerla hasta quedar hermanados, mano que podría recoger brasas sin quemarse y doblar herraduras sin abultar las venas: con tal mano me bendijo y sentí que su ternura colmaba mi cuerpo.

Ahora sé lo que es quedar bendito e ir por el bosque como recién nacido, y dormir confiado como las montañas a la noche, y despertar con el canto de las aves y dar gracias por hallarme otra vez en la luz.

Los de Agubbio se portaron como buenos lobos y cumplieron su promesa, dándome el sustento acordado. Así he envejecido entre el bosque y la ciudadela, yendo y viniendo de las densas hayas a las altas torres, y de las angostas callejuelas a los estrechos barrancos; pero todas las noches me venía a dormir en el abra donde conocí al cordero humano, aquí junto a la piedra donde me dio la mano y bendijo mi corazón.

Con mis viejos músculos que se habían ido entiesando y con estos ojos cansados que ya no podrían distinguir tu silueta, aguardé a que volvieras, Francisco. Por ti encaraba otra y otra mañana. Hasta que comprendí que nunca más nos veríamos en estos espacios, partidos en bosques y en ciudades. Entonces me fui a tender sobre la hierba de nuestro primer encuentro y me dejé enfriar bajo las estrellas.

Los de Agubbio me hallaron, plateado de escarcha, y cuando los vi recogerme con cariño y llevarme hacia la iglesia, les ladré un trueno, antes de correr hacia las estrellas.

Provenza, Francia, 1927

Constant Le Breton, *St. Francis and the Wolf of Gubbio*

CAPÍTULO 4

PETRÓPOLIS, BRASIL, 1943

107

PRAYER TO ST. FRANCIS FOR "YIN"

[affectionate nickname for the poet's nephew, Juan Miguel Godoy]
—composed with the collaboration of the poet's friend, Palma Guillén

St. Francis of Assisi, favorite saint of Juan Miguel, a child saint for bold children and without fraud, as the Lord wants us to be, tell Jesus Christ: here is a child who wants to enter the Heaven of children. With that delicacy that lulled doves to sleep on your dovelike chest, take Juan Miguel for a while and give him the blessed company of your breast. Tell him that you take care of him and guide him. And may your words stay with him like dew on his temples.

St. Francis of Assisi, you knew, as Juan Miguel did, the calls of the world. In your understanding, please intercede for his idle pursuits and plead for his faith as a child, for his forgiveness as a discouraged child. And achieve forgiveness for him, you, who like John the Evangelist and like Peter the Fisherman, you knew what was most hidden, ineffable about the Creator. Ask, then, the one who will deny you nothing: the Forgiving Christ who made you his brother, even to the wounds.

By the bundled veins of the Mystical Body, may your works transfuse, may your merits bleed and be offered to Christ, contributing with your charity to the total redemption of Juan Miguel.

ORACIÓN A SAN FRANCISCO POR "YIN"

[nombre cariñoso del sobrino de GM, Juan Miguel Godoy]
—escrito con la colaboración de Palma Guillén

San Francisco de Asís, santo preferido de Juan Miguel, santo niño para los niños confiados y sin dolo, según nos quiere el Señor; decidle a Jesucristo: Aquí hay un niño que quiere entrar al Cielo de los Niños.

San Francisco de Asís, con esa delicadeza que adormecías palomas sobre tu pecho de palomo, toma un rato a mi Juan Miguel, y dale la compañía bienaventurada de tu pecho. Dile, tú, que lo cuidas y que lo guías. Y tus palabras se le queden como rocío sobre las sienes.

San Francisco de Asís, que conociste como Juan Miguel las llamadas del mundo, comprendiendo intercede por sus devaneos, aboga por su fe de niño, por su perdón de niño descorazonado. Y lógrale el perdón, tú, que como Juan el Evangelista y como Pedro el Pescador, conociste los más recónditos inefables del Creador. Pídele así a quien nada te negará: al Cristo Perdonador con quien hasta en las llagas te hermanaste.

Por la trabazón de las venas del Cuerpo Místico, trasfunde tus obras, sangra tus méritos, y ofrécelos a Cristo, para contribuir con tu caridad a la redención total de Juan Miguel.

Petrópolis, Brasil, 1943

Roberto Montenegro, *De cómo San Francisco sanó a un leproso de cuerpo y de alma*

CAPÍTULO 5

MÉXICO Y WASHINGTON, D.C.

ST. FRANCIS: PATRON SAINT

Gabriela Mistral presented this speech on 12 December 1950 in Washington, D.C., on accepting the Serra Prize of the Academy of Franciscan Historians.

Thank you for the privilege that you have granted me of living an hour among the historians of St. Francis and his American children. And thank you for the superlative honor that you have granted me.

When the world suddenly hardens and becomes a kind of mythological beast rather than the heights of humanity that God wanted, the Franciscan spirit, which is above all a spiritual genius, expands, becoming more robust and it intensifies, as cosmic forces do. A great anxiety takes hold of us and redoubles the meaning of our mission on Earth. Perhaps the meaning of the belt that circles our waist is to remind us every day, especially in catastrophic times, that our mission surrounds us. Spurring us on, it seems to surround us with its urgency, almost like a hemp rope.

In these times, my brothers, we are living in a conflagration that, before it took on the contours of clashing armies, was a dull conflict between peoples, a nightmare of our individual consciences. In peacetime we do not work enough to avoid catastrophe. We slept too long on our society's soft pillow and it is possible that we who pray, who sing our faith, haven't known at nightfall to ask for help as our Holy patron did from the Holy Spirit, which is what we call "inspiration."

In meetings, whether of parliaments or civic elections, ineffective words abound, and illuminating words aren't heeded. Intelligence has never been more present in partisan groups and less present in the divine gift of bringing people together in agreement. In racial and national discussions, empty and arrogant words have overtaken ancient, classical wisdom and austere Christian mercy.

The Mediterranean's ancient paganisms fell despite all of their wisdom about humanity. The new paganisms will also be struck by thunder and lightning. Now the popular images and sacred mysteries of our Holy Patron hover around us and march by our side.

It is time to wake up, to convene the religious consciences of the planet and call on them to re-examine the natural and supernatural life of the patron Saint whom we voluntarily adopt as a standard for living and dying. In this hour of gnashing of teeth, it is good that these images flood our senses and our potentials and that we review some of them even when they are as numerous as the constellations of the sky.

St. Francis was a guardian; he kept watch over all creatures. His language used all the words that speak of love, care, and watchful concern, of help in

SAN FRANCISCO: SANTO PATRONO

Discurso al recibir el premio Serra de las Américas de la Academia Franciscana de la Historia

Gracias a vosotros por el privilegio que me concedéis de vivir una hora entre los historiadores de San Francisco y entre sus hijos americanos. Y gracias por el honor superlativo que me habéis concedido.

Cuando el mundo repentinamente se endurece y se torna en una especie de fiera mitológica en vez de la consumada humanidad que Dios deseara, el genio franciscano, que es sobre todo un genio espiritual, se expande, se hace más sólido y se intensifica como lo hacen las fuerzas cósmicas. Una gran ansiedad se apodera de nosotros y duplica el sentido de nuestra misión terrestre. Posiblemente el significado del cinto que ciñe nuestra cintura sea para recordarnos cada día, y más especialmente en las horas catastróficas, que nuestra misión nos rodea, nos aguijonea y parece cercarnos con su urgencia casi como una cuerda de cáñamo.

Vivimos en estas horas, hermanos míos, una conflagración que, antes de que asumiera contornos de choques de ejércitos, fue un sordo conflicto de pueblos, una pesadilla de nuestras conciencias individuales. No nos esforzamos lo suficiente en tiempo de paz para evitar la hecatombe; dormimos demasiado tiempo sobre la suave almohada de nuestra sociedad y posiblemente nosotros, que oramos, que cantamos nuestra fe, no hemos sabido al caer la noche pedir, como lo hizo nuestro Santo Patrono, la ayuda del Espíritu Santo, a la que damos el nombre de "inspiración".

En las asambleas, llámese parlamentos o comicios cívicos, la palabra inoficiosa abunda y la palabra iluminadora no es escuchada. La inteligencia jamás fue más abundante en grupos partidistas y menos presente en el divino don de traer a los hombres un acuerdo. La palabra hueca y altanera ha reemplazado en las discusiones raciales y nacionales la antigua prudencia clásica y la austera clemencia cristiana.

Los antiguos paganismos del Mediterráneo cayeron, pese a toda su sabiduría en materias humanas, y los nuevos paganismos también serán abatidos por el rayo y el trueno. Las populares imágenes y misterios sagrados de nuestro Santo Patrono revolotean en torno a nosotros en estas horas y marchan al lado nuestro.

Es la hora del despertar, que convoca a las conciencias religiosas del Planeta y las exhorta a un re-examen de la vida natural y sobrenatural del Santo Patrono que voluntariamente adoptamos como norma de vida y de muerte. Está bien que en esta hora de rechinar de dientes inundemos nuestros sentidos

adversity and remorse. At same time, these words are action, for he had the presence and sympathy, the tenderness, the passion and burning fire that constitute the full range of love.

And because of this multitude of extremely human images, artists from all over the globe have fervently devoted themselves to recapturing his form and expression, his Beatitude, prayer and work, his travels and detention, narrow cell and inclement weather. Divine magic sculpted the frieze of his life, at once wandering and intentional. His ambition, transformed by his passion, was one and the same.

St. Francis witnessed the struggles of the Middle Ages without catching their fever. He is the wanderer from all of the paths of Umbria; we see him walking and we see everything that he meets along his road. Here he offered shelter and comfort, in the beyond he settled conflicts, and he cured human ills without causing humiliation. He corrected without the brusqueness of so-called holy wrath.

St. Francis was extremely sensitive. In him, the five senses were divine. He touched carrion without repulsion; he treated both high-ranking and vulgar people as his equals; he gamely breathed in the aromas of Umbria and without averting his face, he mingled with the crowds in the market square. Nor was he irritated by the bluster of powerful people. And he went even further yet, although neither his priors nor his brothers asked him to. He lovingly tended animals, birds, and plants. He found it to be the most natural thing in the world to approach wild beasts, to care for bees, to cover the falcon, to sing; yes, to sing in exquisite Latin verses to the sun, water, and fire and even praise for what we call "inanimate" in a kind of filial love for that Planet that he regarded as a participant in the Divinity, because Christ Our Lord was worthy of coming down to redeem them, first with his Blood and then with his Grace.

It is necessary that we Christians try, from now on, to approach the Asian soul, to cross that tremendous geographical and moral abyss. Courage can work miracles when a supernatural impulse pushes. There is no pagan soldier who approximates the heroism of the Christian one, like St. Francis, who seeks neither profit nor revenge, but rather a precise and unwavering justice.

y nuestras potencialidades con estas imágenes y que pasemos revista a algunas de ellas, aún cuando son tan numerosas como las constelaciones.

San Francisco fue un guardián; mantuvo vigilancia sobre todas las criaturas. Su lenguaje utilizó todas las palabras que hablan de amor, de atención, de vigilante preocupación, de ayuda en la adversidad y de compunción. Pero estas palabras constituyeron, al mismo tiempo, acción, puesto que tuvo la presencia y la simpatía, la ternura, el fervor y el fuego ardiente que constituyen la gama íntegra del amor.

Y, por esta multitud de humanísimas imágenes, los artistas de todo el mundo se han consagrado fervorosamente a recapturar su forma y su expresión. Su beatitud, su oración y su labor, sus andanzas y sus arrestos, la celda cerrada y el tiempo inclemente. La magia divina esculpió el friso de su vida, ambulatoria y al mismo tiempo fijada a un objetivo. Su ambición, alterada por su pasión, era una y la misma.

San Francisco presenció las luchas de la Edad Media sin contagiarse con su fiebre. Es el vagabundo de todos los senderos de Umbría; le vemos caminando y vemos todo lo que encuentra en su camino. Aquí dio refugio y consuelo, más allá solucionó conflictos, remedió humanas miserias sin causar humillación; corrigió sin brusquedad de la llamada "ira santa".

San Francisco era de una sensibilidad extremada. En él, los cincos sentidos eran divinos. Tocaba la carroña sin repulsión; consideraba su igual al de elevada alcurnia y al vulgar; respiraba animosamente los aromas de la Umbría y sin volver la cara se mezclaba con el populacho de la plaza del mercado. Tampoco se airaba ante las bravatas de los poderosos. Y llegaba aún más lejos, aunque ni sus priores ni sus hermanos se lo hubiesen pedido. Cuidaba afectuosamente de animales, aves y plantas. Encontraba la cosa más natural del mundo aproximarse a las bestias salvajes, cuidar de las abejas, amparar al halcón, cantar; sí, cantar, en exquisitos versos latinos al sol, al agua y al fuego y aún alabar aquello que llamamos "inanimado", en una especie de amor filial hacia aquel Planeta que consideraba como partícipe de la Divinidad, porque Cristo N. Señor se dignó descender a él para redimirlos primero con su Sangre y luego con su Gracia.

Es preciso que nosotros los cristianos tratemos a partir de ahora de aproximarnos al alma asiática, salvar aquel tremendo abismo geográfico y moral. El valor es capaz de milagros, cuando surge con impulso sobrenatural. No hay soldado pagano que alcance el heroísmo del cristiano, cual San Francisco, no busca el provecho ni la venganza, sino más bien una justicia exacta e indudable.

México y/o Estados Unidos, nov.–dic. 1950

Roberto Montenegro, *Parábola del grano de mostaza*

motivos

THE LIFE OF ST. FRANCIS

AFTERWORD

Name Abbreviations

AR	Alfonso Reyes
BC	Benjamín Carrión
CEE	Carmela Echenique de Errázuriz
CP	Carlos Pellicer
EB	Eduardo Barrios
EL	Eugenio Labarca
FHC	Federico Henríquez Carvajal
FM	Francis de Miomandre
GM	Gabriela Mistral
GZ	Gonzalo Zaldumbide
JGM	Joaquín García Monge
JI	Juana de Ibarbourou
JT	Julio Torri
JV	José Vasconcelos
L	Lucila
LG	Lucila Godoy
LVS	Luis Vargas Saavedra
MG	Manuel Gómez Morín
MGM	Manuel Guzmán Maturana
MFGH	María Luisa Fernández de García-Huidobro
MMM	Manuel Magallanes Moure
MR	Manuela Reyes
MSM	Maximiliano Salas Marchán
OET	Olaya Errázuriz de Tomic
PAC	Pedro Aguirre Cerda
PG	Palma Guillén [de Nicolau]
PM	Pedro Moral
PP	Pedro Prado
RT	Radomiro Tomic
TML	Teresa María Llona
VGH	Vicente Huidobro

HOW LUCILA GODOY BECAME GABRIELA MISTRAL

Strange Fame and Queer Poetics: The Saint's Life

Ironies pervade the fame of the first Latin American to win the Nobel Prize in Literature (1945), a poet, journalist, and diplomat who wrote under the invented name and literary identity of Gabriela Mistral. She is revered as an educator, yet teachers hounded her from schools in her native Chile. She never bore children, yet governments promoted her as a figure of motherhood and charity, ignoring her immense volume of writing. She became a symbol of the Americas, yet she lived almost twenty years in Europe. In 1935 a special act of the Chilean legislature supposedly freed her to serve as a consul of Chile wherever she chose, yet politics demanded her near-constant travel. This international celebrity and confidante of presidents and senators lived under intense media scrutiny, yet she maintained many secrets: unexplained trips, swift changes of residence, and a boy whom she raised as a son.

Many contradictions surround Gabriela Mistral. Few are more puzzling than her relation to organized religion and its explosive intersection with politics. As politics pushed the poet into uncomfortable allegiances, she began writing what she called "heroic biographies." The first ones appeared as parables from the past with clear application to the present. Writing biographies often helped her to avoid speaking unwisely when silence was not an option. The first and longest of her heroic biographies was the poetic "life" of St. Francis of Assisi. In her process of composition, she turned to the literary genre of *motivos*. In the literary creation of the time, "motivos" alludes to "a contemplated reality that moves into writing as that reality sparks a poetic idea whose force channeled into prose or verse comments on it, sentimentally" (Barca lxxix).

When Gabriela Mistral began writing the biography of St. Francis, she had recently moved to live and work in postrevolutionary Mexico. She had reached the end of her tether in her native Chile, where she had been the target of repeated public attacks. She sought and accepted a commission from the Mexican government, and she arrived in Mexico in July of 1922. There the poet worked with an unparalleled group of young artists, writers, and politicians, mostly revolutionaries, Marxist and otherwise, producing murals, magazines, books, theater, and film. Funding all of this was the office of the flamboyant José Vasconcelos, who headed up the newly organized Secretariat of Education, Culture, and Indigenous Affairs (SEP).

Standard portraits of Gabriela Mistral's life and work in Mexico follow the "great man" approach of describing her relation to that country primarily in terms of her relation to José Vasconcelos. By contrast, the present text draws from contemporaneous materials to show the poet's complex relations across a wide-ranging group of artists, politicians, and intellectuals within Mexico and extending to its diaspora. She regularly interacted with the muralists Diego Rivera and his lesser-known colleague, the painter Roberto Montenegro. Mistral also collaborated with many diplomats and writers and with the poets who subsequently have become known as "Los Contemporáneos." As the poet's efficient longtime companion, the Mexican diplomat Palma Guillén worked to suppress the evidence of these and other associations, and the present text is the first to outline this important network of friendships, which extended far beyond the nation's borders.

A great biographer of José Vasconcelos, the Mexican writer José Joaquín Blanco, has stated that "Mexico was a university education for Gabriela Mistral" (107). Mexico also brought celebrity to Mistral. She became a major Latin American writer and public figure. In Mexico, the future Nobel laureate experienced a transformation of her political, religious, and artistic perspectives. Mexico's impact on Gabriela Mistral first becomes evident in her strange and beautiful *Motivos de San Francisco*, which she began writing five months after she had arrived in Mexico. Neither the genre of biography nor the saint's life had previously interested her,[1] yet her experiences in Mexico led her to plan out a series of "heroic biographies," beginning with this one and extending to Sor Juana, Vasco de Quiroga, Dante, and Tolstoy. She soon made the form of the heroic biography, profile, or sketch into a signature mode within her journalism.

Stylistic influences on this "life" begin with *modernismo*, Latin America's unique variant on Symbolist poetry. Long before she left Chile for Mexico in 1922, much of the poetry and prose that Gabriela Mistral had written blended *modernismo* with theosophy. The latter was a worldwide fellowship self-positioned between religion and science. Queer- and woman-friendly lodges published magazines and loaned theosophical texts drawn from Eastern and other esoteric sources. The poet combined her readings from theosophy and *modernismo* to develop an erotic closeted poetics that informed much of her first volume of poetry, *Desolación* (1922) (Horan, "Alternative"). That queer poetics, appropriate to her circumstances as a public schoolteacher from the provincial lower middle class, persisted in her work following her move to

Mexico. Her writing shortly began to register Mexico's social unrest. Yet her poetic prose, and particularly her *Motivos*, her life of St. Francis, continued what she had developed in that earlier combination of theosophy and *modernismo*. Reflecting her return or conversion to Catholicism, to the atmosphere of heightened emotion from her previous style, she added a new, deep, intense, sensual pleasure in nature and in folk arts, and an awakened social awareness.

Religion and Politics

The religious identifications of Gabriela Mistral have long been subject to speculation and debate (Taylor; Vargas Saavedra, "Introducción"). She has been variously claimed as a Catholic—the religion into which she was baptized and confirmed as a child—and a theosophist, dating from about 1911. Her experiences in Chile made her reticent on the subject of religious belief, for she owed her career and early publication opportunities to politicians in Chile's avowedly anti-clerical Radical Party. As she walked a fine line between Conservatives and Radicals, her published writings avoided overt Christian references. By 1920, however, she described herself as "Christian but not Catholic" (GM [LG] to PAC, 1920).* All of this would change, most improbably, when the poet left Chile for Mexico, where her growing social awareness became evident in what she subsequently called "Cristianismo con sentido social."

Gabriela Mistral's change of consciousness set her on a collision course with world politics. On arriving in Mussolini's Italy in 1924, for instance, she was outspoken in condemning fascism even as she headed to Assisi and began the process of becoming a Third-Order lay Franciscan. The next events proved more difficult yet: in 1926, Mexico's new government launched a systematic repression of Catholicism. Churches were closed. Priests were fined and jailed. None of the poet's Mexican friends, even avowed Catholics such as Palma Guillén and Manuel Gómez Morín, dared denounce this. They remained silent throughout the subsequent revolt, called the "Cristero War," in which some 90,000 federal troops and peasants died, decimating Mexico's agricultural heartlands. Despite circumstances that suddenly and suspiciously narrowed Gabriela Mistral's access to newspaper publication, she questioned the Mexican government's handling of the rebellion. She also returned to literature, turning her anguish into further episodes in the life of St. Francis. The combined circumstances of the Cristero War in Mexico and the dictatorship in Chile deepened Gabriela Mistral's commitment to remaining in Europe while writing about the Americas.

*Please see p. 118 for a list of abbreviations of names.

Gabriela Mistral, about 1917, Los Andes, Chile

Memories of Childhood

Born into poverty as Lucila Godoy Alcayaga in 1889, the writer grew up in the remote Andean village of Montegrande in the Valley of Elqui. One of several narrow, semitropical valley oases, the Valley of Elqui is formed by Andean snowmelt that waters and cuts through parched lands en route to the Pacific Ocean. To the north is the Atacama Desert. Chile's Central Valley lies 500 kilometers to the south.

Evoking the idyllic qualities of her earliest childhood in "Recuerdo de la madre ausente," the poet recalled days spent in a Franciscan communion with nature. Her mother, Petronila or "Petita" Alcayaga, was often alarmed to discover Lucila "chatting with the twisted grape stalks and with a slender, fine almond tree that resembled an entranced boy" (GM, comp., *Lecturas* 12). Lucila learned to read and write from her generous older half sister, Emelina Molina, a village schoolteacher, whose wages supported the small family. No such help came from Jerónimo Godoy, the girl's father. A sporadically employed, bohemian schoolteacher and guitar player, he had long since abandoned them. Decades later, she wrote frankly of his absence: "My father came and went from Atacama to the Valley of Elqui. He never talked about his life in his province. He had already gone over to liquor and my mother and my sister were only relieved when he left" (GM to RT, Feb. 1954).

As an adult, Gabriela Mistral developed a vast repertoire of autobiographical speeches and writings that developed her persona as a rustic, self-taught poet and social reformer. She turned her traumatic experiences with formal education into a mantra. Her most frequently repeated episode recreated the beginning and end of her formal schooling. The drama opened innocently enough: her sister Emelina conceived "una idea peregrina," a far-fetched plan (GM to PM, June 1948). The family would move from the village of Montegrande into the provincial town of Vicuña, following the narrow river valley to where the flood plain spreads out approaching the ocean. The little Lucila, boarding with friends, was to attend and complete Vicuña's primary school under the protection of the school's director, Doña Adelaida Olivares, her confirmation godmother. That old woman, highly religious and half-blind, made the youngster into her *lazarillo* and put her in charge of distributing paper supplies to her fellow students. This posed a problem that the poet described in an interview with the Argentine writer María Rosa Oliver: "I was more than timid; I had no character whatsoever, and the students took as much paper as they wanted from me, so that the supply was gone in eight months or less. When the Director asked the class why the paper was all gone, my school friends declared that I was the guilty one, as they hadn't received any but the correct amount" (GM, "Autobiografía," 1941). Adelaida Olivares made inquiries and unjustly denounced the ten-year-old Lucila as a thief. The other students confronted and threw stones at the innocent newcomer, who crept away, bruised and mute, from the town's pretty, flower-strewn plaza. When Lucila's mother protested, Olivares answered that the shy girl was mentally disabled, for she could barely stutter out her name, "Totilla Loloy." "Keep her at home and teach her chores," the teacher advised (Horan, Interview, Doris Dana). But the girl silently rebelled. "If they think I'll be useful around the house, I'm lost. So I sat by the stove with my notebooks, to dream" (GM, Interview 1954? qtd. in Spinola).

A Struggling Adolescent

The girl's family slid further into poverty. Although they moved every year or more, hoping for a better situation, they remained in or near the rural Valley of Elqui. Petronila Alcayaga soon decided that Lucila would follow her father, sister, and two aunts by becoming a teacher. In that first job, the fifteen-year-old Lucila worked as a teacher's aide in a rural school by the ocean at the rural edges of the provincial and ecclesiastical capital of La Serena. The difficulties that she faced in these early years as a teacher and writer formed the basis of Gabriela Mistral's autobiographical essay "El oficio lateral" (1949), which alludes to the class prejudice that she repeatedly encountered:

> I didn't hit it off with the Director. It seems that I didn't have the happy and easy character that wins people over. My boss put up with me and I put up with her . . . the big boys in the school gave me a certain defense against the thundering voice of the Boss and her great disdain as a well-dressed woman toward her helper with an ugly blouse and fat shoes. . . . [Softening the poet's memory was the school's seaside location in the middle of a huge olive grove.] The slightest stuttering of the forest's speech keeps me for days and months. (43, 45)

In contrast to these hostile encounters with educators, the teenager's chance meetings with editors and politicians opened new opportunities in this province of her childhood and adolescence. Her "Oficio lateral" recounts how "an old journalist and I ran into one another" (43). Bernardo Ossandón, publisher of several local newspapers, loaned her books from "the Ali Baba's cave, the treasure" of his provincial library: "it was my Paris in Miniature, my Rome in eight meters squared," she recalled (GM to Alone, 1930?).

The subjectivity of the poet's account, stressing trauma, lost innocence, and lasting gratitude, skips over important political factors that became a lifelong aspect of her difficult relation with her native land. Ossandón was a leading Mason and influential member of Chile's Radical, that is, anti-clerical, pro-secular political party. He published newspapers that followed the Radical agenda. As opposed to the Conservatives, the party of large landowners, who bought votes by the truckload, the Radicals courted favor by serving as a generalized employment agency, especially for teachers. Ossandón's active patronage helps explain the changing fortunes of the fifteen-year-old Lucila Godoy, whose formal education had ended before she had turned twelve. Through Ossandón and his friends, the girl managed to get work as a teacher. Her persistence mattered, as she accepted jobs in rural schools that credentialed educators had snubbed. She had only the publication of her overblown, sometimes incoherent writings to stand in for the teaching credential, the piece of paper that she lacked.

Early Publications and New Setbacks

The novice teacher and writer had been publishing in Ossandón's Radical newspapers for little over a year when a pseudonymous reader wrote in to complain, describing her work as the product of "a mind unbalanced, perhaps . . . by thinking too much" (Madac). As poems from local admirers poured in, her next essays were less emotionally based, with front-page coverage. She advocated scientific study and the education of women (GM, "La instrucción"). Like many an ambitious, "artistic," but poor and thus unmarriageable young woman living in the provinces, she showed interest in the wider world. Her writing reflected what Hispanist Noël Valis, focusing on Spain but with relevance to nineteenth- and twentieth-century Latin America, has termed "the culture of cursilería." The strangeness of Gabriela Mistral began and remained faithfully "cursi" (kitschy), in an incongruous mixture of provincial and cosmopolitan, romantic and modern.

Within the provincial city of La Serena, local educators implacably opposed Lucila Godoy's efforts to train as a teacher. Friends helped her obtain a semi-clerical appointment in the city's privately run Liceo de Niñas. Here she clashed with the director, Ana Krause, whom the poet later described as "an extraordinary German woman . . . who ran the school half-ways between a barracks and a workshop" and whose staff "obeyed her with an almost irrational, mythological respect" (GM, "Autobiografía," 1941). It is not clear why Krause forced the young woman's resignation at year's end. The poet assigned various reasons, depending on where, when, and to whom she narrated the episode. In some versions, Lucila was dismissed for having conspired to admit girls from impoverished families. In other accounts, the authorities feared her as a potential leader. In still other retellings, a former classmate relayed her reputation as a thief. Or the headmistress despised her as a fool, as the poet eventually admitted to her ignorance. "I knew very little about official writing and perhaps about any kind of writing although I was already publishing in newspapers. The humble provincial newspapers receive and publish almost everything" (ibid.).

Despite Lucila Godoy's struggles in the conservative, class-conscious environment, she continued to get jobs as an itinerant educator. Success came from her "side work." She published at least eighty-five different pieces in the province's newspapers and worked at four different schools before she turned twenty-two and moved away from the province where she had been born and raised (Manzano). Ironically, those very publications proved an obstacle when she sought admission to the local normal school. She had completed the required exams and showed evidence of her teaching experience but she was excluded. No explanation was offered. Only later, as she explained to Pedro Aguirre Cerda, the Radical politician and future president of Chile who became her steadiest patron, did she learn that the school's chaplain, Father Ignacio Munizaga, had lobbied against her.

> [I]n a silent intrigue aimed at getting rid of me for having been seen reading and having others read some scientific works that a well-read man in my town got for me: don Bernardo Ossandón. . . . I was already writing in the Radical newspaper *El Coquimbo* and tended to be overly sincere in describing my ideas, which weren't irreligious, but religious in a sense different from the current one. (GM [LG] to PAC, 1920)

A chance meeting again intervened in her favor. Dismissed from the Liceo and barred from the normal school, Lucila Godoy was boarding a train at the port of Coquimbo in order to return to the Valley of Elqui. Boarding with her was an old former governor of the province. Her seatmate nodded as they passed La Cantera, a group of shacks scattered across the dunes, a stone's throw from the ocean. There was scant running water or vegetation, but the girl took the job he offered her developing a kind of night school for workers. Years later she fondly looked back on how she would sit around swapping stories with the teenagers and illiterate adults who paid her a kind of tithe in harvested vegetables (qtd. in Spinola). When the train stopped, she would pick up and drop off her publications, which were now circulating throughout the province. Both in the shacks by the ocean and in her next post, further inland but in the same province and on the rail line, she began signing herself "Gabriela Mistral." Her literary name referred both to the Messenger Archangel Gabriel, bringer of good news to humankind, and to the mistral, the cold north wind that howls across southern France (and elsewhere on the Mediterranean).

In adopting this invented name, "Gabriela Mistral," the writer abandoned her earlier, vaguely allegorical pseudonyms of "Alguien" or "Soledad." She borrowed the authority of two male European regional and romantic Mediterranean writers, Frederic Mistral of Provence and the Italian Gabriele D'Annunzio. She differed from her later student and friend Pablo Neruda, the former Nephtalí Reyes, in that she never officially dropped the "Lucila Godoy" of her civil name: it faded from view, reserved to consular and other official papers.

That earlier name sometimes surfaced at the foot of letters to patrons humbly requesting favors, such as a loan. Or she would instruct correspondents to use it when gossips and mail-thieves lurked nearby. "*L*" became her talisman for the clandestine, as the poet Gonzalo Rojas, a later admirer, wrote after her death:

> ending
> less with the L of the famous lucidity
> than with this other L
> of liberty
> of locura
> that illuminates
> the depth
> of the lugubrious
> of the labyrinth
> Lambda
> loony
> batty
> before the flaming match
> long before
> the whip-stroke
> of the Logos (Rojas)

Or the winglike "L" of her secret missives might well mark an entirely fictitious identity.

Walking the Tightrope and Scaling the Ladder: Religious Conflict and the Chilean State

Conflicts over religion in education were something of a birthright for a poet whose very family was divided between Radicals and devout Catholics. Her mother's loose affiliation with the Radical Party put bread on the family table. When her father, a former seminarian, married her mother, he defied his own mother's wishes that he become a priest. The poet's later recollections cast her paternal grandmother, Isabel Villanueva, as a religious fanatic and nearly insane, in "a nervous inheritance that I have resisted, thanks to the will and the ration of good sense coming from my mother" (GM to TML, after 1943). Gabriela Mistral often evoked how her mother sent her off to spend Sunday afternoons with her "crazy grandmother." The old woman undid the ten-year-old girl's careful curls before directing her to take "an enormous Bible" from the shelf and read aloud from the Psalms in "an endless stream" of which the girl understood little or nothing (GM, "Mi experiencia"). Isabel's Bible-reading was, she observed, otherwise unheard-of among the province's women. Eventually the poet's stories of Isabel Villanueva formed the basis of her claiming

Jewish ancestry, which Gabriela Mistral supported by citing her grandmother's surname, "Villanueva," common among *conversos*.

Despite the poet's later memories, the evidence is clear: poetry and novels captured her adolescent imagination, while religion and the Bible interested her not at all. In her earliest extant notebook, from 1907, she studiously copied out only verses from profane writers such as Victor Hugo, Edgar Allen Poe, Rubén Darío and Vargas Vila, the Colombian writer of potboilers (Rama). None of her (abundant) early publications register the slightest interest in or evidence of any kind of Biblical influence (GM, *GM en La Voz*). Her great concerns were her two professions of writing and teaching.

Prompted by friends, the writer was twenty-one years old when she traveled to Santiago, where she passed equivalency exams that qualified her to teach at the secondary level. In the following year of 1911, she moved to the northern desert port city of Antofagasta, a booming mining center full of nouveau riche. Here the schoolteacher-poet joined a lodge of theosophists. This loosely organized worldwide brotherhood attracted literary people in Chile, other parts of Latin America, Europe, the United States, and India. Theosophy offered a spiritual life independent of the more established religions' entrenched hierarchies. Consistent with the poet's later Franciscanism, it encouraged her meditation on sentient, nonhuman consciousness, including the world of plants. The Buddhism that she later claimed to have practiced in her years as an itinerant rural schoolteacher likely began in theosophy: "From twenty to thirty years of age I was a Buddhist, hidden from people. I hid my belief as one hides a wound because I was a state-employed schoolteacher and because I divined—as I now know—that it's a tragedy to be that amid a people that is or may be Catholic or idolatrously Catholic" (GM to GZ, 1934).

The poet's next move in her teaching career brought her to the mining and transportation hub of Los Andes, a half-day's easy travel to Chile's capital of Santiago. Mistral's published materials of the time showed that she developed ideas from theosophy that were consonant with Christianity and Masonry, such as the idealization of the spiritual teacher as a moral guide or guru. In addition, her own serious bearing, mixing warmth and mystery, made religious skeptics such as Manuel Guzmán Maturana, a prominent Chilean editor, educator, and Masonic "grand master," regard her as something of a spiritual teacher. Despite the difference in their ages—she was just twenty-five and not yet famous—Guzmán Maturana breaks off his detailed instructions about her contributions to a textbook and seems half-jokingly to refer to her as a guru: "Jesus, Buddha! About the latter, you will have to instruct me" (MGM to GM, July 1914).

Gabriela Mistral's residence in the mountain stronghold of Los Andes, near Santiago, brought many opportunities to publish in magazines and textbooks. At first, educators and theosophists warmly greeted her writing's proposal of a generalized nonsectarian brotherhood. By at least 1916, however, urban educators began to squeeze her out. The new fashion and zeal for "laboratory empiricism" did not square with the poet's spiritual and rustic self-fashioning as a "teacher who's almost a peasant," as Gabriela Mistral proposed in the following speech aimed at teachers, which she drafted but did not publish:

> [A] class is pure poetry when one explains the Sermon on the Mount with the soul, with all of the soul. Because to teach this one must have Christ in one's heart, being somewhat Franciscan, or like Teresa of Ávila, that is, a poet. . . . Who is the most saintly man? The one who loves the most, whose mouth remembers nature, always at the tip of the tongue to offer a kiss, the one who most deeply has the gift of sympathy for what lives. A true poet is this. The trembling of a breeze across the grass shakes him like wind and a shout of human pain, like a hurricane. (GM, "La enseñanza" 275)

Such sensuality, decadence, and idealism were sorely tested when Gabriela Mistral managed to enter school administration. In the meantime, she taught school and wrote letters from her rented rooms in Los Andes. Her window looked onto the road to Mendoza, Argentina. The Trans-Andean Railway rumbled close by and the Aconcagua River flowed in the distance. Thinking of these wider horizons, she began corresponding with some of the most noted writers of her time. She began with Rubén Darío and Amado Nervo, who both fed her interest in Franciscanism and in the world.

Franciscan Traditions in Latin American Poetry: Rubén Darío and Amado Nervo (FROM 1912)

The tradition of St. Francis of Assisi in Latin American poetry arguably dates from "Los motivos del lobo," a brilliant narrative poem in which Nicaraguan poet Rubén Darío retold the "Legend of Gubbio's Wolf." The dramatic qualities of Darío's poem made it a staple of poetry recitals for decades. The poet describes a terrified village facing the wolf's ferocious nocturnal raids. These end when St. Francis, the conciliator, befriends the wild animal. As Darío's impersonal narration points out that the savage wolf cannot enter civilization and must return to the forest, the poem denies a soul for the wolf, whose consciousness ends with his death.

In Mistral's prose version of the legend "Un lobo en el cielo," the final episode in her life of St. Francis, the poet extends much further Darío's sympathy for the wolf. Mistral's *motivo* relates the story from the recollected perspective of the wolf, who is moved by the tenderness of Francis, described as a "human lamb" and type of Christ. Now almost domesticated, the wolf faithfully awaits the Saint's return, going out to the margin of the animal and human worlds, "between forests and cities," where the two had first met, hoping to repeat that encounter. When death releases the still-waiting wolf, the villagers bear the corpse into the church in violation of the Christian division between animals and humanity. In a sign of Mistral's continued absorption in theosophy and reincarnation, her retelling has the animal's spirit racing off in a thunderclap "to the stars."

After years of having read and admired the work of Rubén Darío, the Chilean poet sent him a letter shortly after her move to Los Andes in 1912. She opened this first letter expressing her disappointment to learn that his planned visit to Chile had been cancelled. Describing herself as "a schoolteacher at the foot of the Andes," she conveyed enthusiasm for his verses. She enclosed her poem "El ángel guardián" along with a prose fable, "La defensa de la belleza." Darío's Paris-based magazine *Elegancias* published both, bringing Mistral her first international recognition (Belmas 155-64).

Mistral's other exchanges of letters from Los Andes present multiple samples of her writing about love from the oddly detached "outsider" perspective. Among her correspondents was the forty-six-year-old Mexican poet Amado Nervo, who was then regarded as Darío's most likely successor. Mistral's contact with Nervo commenced shortly after Darío died from complications of alcoholism in 1916. She told a friend that what most interested her about Nervo was "less his literature than his soul." She eulogized Darío as a "pagan, seven times a pagan" while the living Nervo struck her as a "suffering and serene mystic" and "el Tagore de América" (GM to EL, Mar. 1916, 31).

Nervo's reputation in his lifetime and after his premature death in 1919 reflects the ebbs and flows of twentieth-century acceptance of same-sex attraction and gender equality. For decades the Mexican writer and diplomat was "the one poet most frequently read by the women of América" (Iglesias 50). Fifty years after his death he seemed headed for oblivion until critics began to recognize him as an important precursor in writing of the gothic, the fantastic, and queer desire (Leal 489-93, Molloy 203-13, Chaves 275-85). As the twenty-first century began, writer Roberto Bolaño summed up this new appreciation: "[W]e've had to go back to Nervo to find (whistles), a real poet, a faggot poet" (71).

In Mistral's correspondence it is clear that what she found attractive in Nervo was his writing about love and loss. She mimicked the closeted quality of Nervo's spiritual love poetry when she reported having told him that his verses taught her "how to love, and then, after love disappeared, to express sorrow, in a restrained and acerbic way" (GM to EL, 1916). References in her letters and poetry suggest that reading Nervo encouraged her to develop a cosmopolitan and mystical perspective that employed the themes of the absent lover and posthumous love, using the language of spiritualism and theosophy to avoid specifying the gender of the beloved. She told Nervo that she identified this gender-indeterminate love as Franciscan: "I feel your heart in every verse, lighter than a dove, freed to passion in unheard of ways . . . I am saddened by this seraphic verse that seems to tell me: the breast from which I have departed is as foreign to yours as to Francis's itself" (qtd. in Loveluck 504).

Gabriela Mistral ensured the Mexican poet-diplomat's attention in her frank political awareness from her very first letter's mention of "the painful news from Mexico . . . in this bitter hour" (ibid., 502). Mexico was in chaos. Insurgents battled over the capital and US troops had repeatedly entered Mexican territory. Mistral's next letter expressed a manifestly anti-imperialist perspective in her reports of contacts with sympathetic writers from Argentina and her offer to help promote Mexico's image. "The Mexicans are a great people," she told him, "and if the Yankees present them as puppets in magazines and newspapers it's because they want to pardon their fifteen years of pressure on a great, unfortunate country" (ibid., 508).

As Mistral's combining of poetry and politics in these letters virtually guaranteed Nervo's grateful response, they corresponded for three years, with their friendship cut short by Nervo's sudden death in 1919. Mistral's contact with the Mexican poet-diplomat nonetheless strongly impacted her life and thought. Through Nervo, Mistral met his closest colleague, another poet-diplomat, Enrique González Martínez, who began serving as Mexican minister, that is, ambassador to Chile in 1920. He is most broadly remembered, however, within the first generation of poets after *modernismo*. He urged others to join him in "twisting the swan's neck" of Darío-inspired modernist decadence. González Martínez supplied the necessary introductions and recommendations when Mistral signaled her interest in traveling to Mexico. Before that happened, however, it is useful to know what opportunities came to her in Chile.

Correspondents within Chile: Manuel Magallanes and Eduardo Barrios (FROM 1914)

The schoolteacher-poet's spunk in contacting foreign poets such as Darío and Nervo from her residence in Los Andes did not apply to nearby Santiago. In a letter from 1912 she explained her caution: "When I go to the capital I avoid the visits of the very writers with whom I maintain correspondence, because, in reality, they inspire in me a great literary, but not always personal admiration. They don't inspire in me that full confidence that I need in order to visit a house" (GM to Ossandón de la Peña, 12 Oct. 1912). Her caution was justified. Gender roles and differences in social class proved insurmountable in one such relation, with Manuel Magallanes Moure, one of Chile's most influential poets. Although he acknowledged her talent in awarding her the top prize in a nationwide poetry contest, "Los juegos florales," his surviving letters testify to his difficulty in regarding women as his intellectual equals: "In all of Spanish America," he told her, she stood apart. "I've never been able to take seriously the rest of the women who do verse in Indo-Spanish lands." He observed that few women "knew how to express their emotions" (MMM to LG, 1 Mar. 1915).

Magallanes was thirty-six, while Lucila was twenty-four when the correspondence began. He stood many ranks above her in social status. Each had spent many years honing their skills in correspondence. As a teenager, he had used clandestine correspondence to evade parental prohibitions on courting his wealthy first cousin, thirteen years his senior. After a few years of happy marriage with that cousin, he began falling in and out of love with various women to whom he dedicated and published poems, minimally disguising the beloveds' identities (Redondo Magallanes).

Lucila/Gabriela and Manuel commenced a bizarre exchange that eventually stretched, by her later account, into "hundreds of letters." It seems that the two writers disguised their identities in order to avoid discovery. For years, she refused to meet him. When he predictably lost interest, she apparently rekindled the relationship by claiming to have fallen in love with him. A sense of counterfeit emotion pervades many of the letters, with their torrid promises, recriminations, and assertions of her coarseness versus his blue-blooded refinement. The terse statements of disappointment that she recorded in her notebooks seem far more real. She headed one page "1916, Copa de Rocío." On the facing page she wrote, "1917, Vaso de Amargura."

Gabriela/Lucila managed at least one stable alliance, with the Chilean novelist Eduardo Barrios, a lower-level bureaucrat who shared her precariously middle-class status and condition as an outsider in Santiago. Together they navigated the rich yet treacherous world of bohemian Santiago. Her letters to him adopt a familiar, often jocular tone: she calls him "little brother." While the correspondence eventually spanned several decades, their friendship's earliest years seem to be the more revealing of their mutual support. Barrios interceded for her among authorities in Chile and poured time into editing her work. She promoted his novels and relayed amusing anecdotes that contained gossip useful to advancing his career.

Barrios's widely published Franciscan novel *El hermano asno* (1923) directly influenced Mistral's interest in Francis of Assisi. Barrios set the novel in downtown Santiago's Franciscan monastery. The central character, Friar Rufino, gradually loses his reputation for holiness when he refuses to deny rumors that he has had sexual relations with a woman who visits the monastery. Mistral rightly regarded the novel as a masterful psychological study: her first full-fledged book review recognized its purity and simplicity of language and style.[2] Shortly after publishing that review, Mistral commenced writing about the life of St. Francis. In a letter to Barrios, she attributed her interest to having read his novel: "Your book stoked the mystical figure in me despite its underlying irony." Although she questioned the novel's ironic ending, she and Barrios shared that self-deprecating, dry mockery of *modernismo*'s contradictory attitudes toward the body, which Francis affectionately termed his "Brother Ass." Where Mistral portrays Francis mistreating his body, her narrator comments: "Yes, Pobrecillo! Everything under the sun has experienced your tenderness except for that body of yours" (Horan, *Motivos* 20). Another irony arises in what Mistral mentioned as one of her favorite scenes in the novel: after Friar Rufino tries and fails to quiet a dog that barks at all passers-by, he abandons his human superiority and joins the animal in barking (GM to EB, 15 Jan. 1923). Barrios's and Mistral's representations of Christianity's interest in the body show their simultaneous development away from *modernismo* into the literary realism that is an ongoing aspect of how religious feeling is represented in Spanish-language prose (Valis, *Sacred Realism*).

Internal Exile: Changing Directions in Punta Arenas (1918–1920)

Gabriela Mistral was still living in Los Andes, where her growing reputation exposed to her to public humiliation. In March and April of 1917, a wealthy would-be critic purchased *Sucesos*, a widely circulating magazine previously friendly to her work. Using the pseudonym "Juan Duval," the critic proceeded to parody her writing. Mistral quickly persuaded friends to defend her in print. She wasted no time in making a formal request to transfer from Los Andes. When the school year ended, she was appointed to direct a failing school in the socially divided city of Punta Arenas, more than 2000 kilometers to the south of Santiago.[3]

The location, close to Cape Horn, was so stunning that no one seems to have noticed, much less complained, about the new director's lack of a teaching degree. She had already risen from teacher's aide in a rural school to service in two different secondary schools. In Punta Arenas, she likely faced no rivals to direct an overcrowded, poorly heated school where medical examinations had just revealed rickets in more than 90 percent of the students. Scarpa's excellent book on her two years in Punta Arenas (*Desterrada*) examines the challenges that she faced and details her published and unpublished work from the time.

The poet's letters and publications from Punta Arenas reveal her keen political skills. She appreciated the area's strategic importance, closer to Buenos Aires than Santiago, in a watery archipelago near the Beagle Channel boundaries disputed with Argentina. The territory was ruled by a series of military governors who came and went. She promised her political mentor in Santiago that once suffrage was extended to the local residents, her students would turn the area into a Radical Party stronghold. (This prediction proved accurate.)

The area's dramatic beauty and high immigrant population appealed to her. The latter made Punta Arenas unusual among Chilean cities. The overwhelming majority of its 20,000 local residents had migrated from elsewhere: Yugoslavia, Spain, the island of Chiloé, Great Britain, Argentina, and Italy. Only the nation's capital boasted more newspapers and magazines, in more languages. The social divides were greater than anywhere else in Chile: Punta Arenas had a large population of millionaires, who owned the vast sheep farms where men, women, and children labored day and night throughout the short Antarctic summer. The new director and her crew of new teachers descended from the boat as summer turned to fall. The wind blew like a charging buffalo. On leaving a reception in their honor at the Hotel Cosmo, they walked out onto the street to encounter, for the first time in their lives, a city blanketed in snow.

The new school director in Punta Arenas found that getting provisions for her school required cultivating both sides of the warring camps in the city, as she explained to her friend Eduardo Barrios back in Santiago. One letter suggests that she courted "both god and the devil, here, with workers (a power center) and the authorities." She seemingly convinced each side—anti-clerical anarchists versus the pious conservatives—that she represented them: "the radicals would see me as Belén de Zarraga [an anarchist freethinker and feminist icon who promoted unions] and the pious people, as pious." She mocked her balancing act: "It's a lot to ask. Belén always struck me as coarse and ridiculous, and as for being pious, it's too hard for me to bend" (GM to EB, Jan.-Feb. 1919).

The writer's range and depth of work grew immensely during her two years in Punta Arenas, which is where she made her first efforts with the *motivo* as a literary form. Drawing on the Bible, she wrote three strange series: "Motivos de la Pasión," "Motivos del barro," and "Poemas del éxtasis." In each, she developed the quasi-Biblical mode of the parable as a moralistic lesson from nature, narrating events from its passive but sentient perspective. Thus the poet writes from the perspective of the olive trees in Gethsemane, relating their shocked witness to the scene of Judas's betraying Jesus with a kiss that forever profanes all subsequent kisses. In "Motivos del barro" she expresses profane love from the perspectives of mud or clay, describing its inchoate longing to be touched, formed, shaped into vessels that can be filled. In all of these *motivos*, the poet infuses the natural world with the possibility of mutual sympathy and recognition. These early *motivos* illuminate an intense inner world struggling toward expression that animates the vegetable and mineral realms in a concern that remains constant throughout her poetry.

The extremes of the surrounding environment that the poet encountered in Chile's far south marked much of her work at this time. As had become her custom, she retreated to the countryside over the Christmas vacation. New surroundings usually encouraged her to experiment with new forms, and she had no shortage of venues in which to publish. As her accomplishments produced other offers of employment in Buenos Aires, she threatened to accept the job and move unless Santiago transferred her to a warmer clime, less ruinous to her health.

Campaigning in Temuco for a Post in Santiago (EARLY 1921)

Gabriela Mistral's move to the rainy, semi-frontier town of Temuco disappointed her: she told friends that she found it inferior to Punta Arenas. Developed on lands seized from indigenous people just two generations earlier, Temuco was little more than a military garrison and trading outpost. In moving to direct yet another "failing" school, she encountered "near guerrilla warfare" in both her workplace and in the town. On the one hand, she would renew and make new friendships, such as the one with a fifteen-year-old poet who had begun publishing verses as Pablo Neruda. She found, on the other hand, that the area's rigged elections meant that the local senator would be, incredibly, the very "Juan Duval" who had earlier attacked and humiliated her in the Santiago press. As this dashed every hope of obtaining advantages for her school, she weighed how she might leave. As she had now directed two failing schools, and had been teaching for over fifteen years, she made a bid for the choicest of vacancies. Were she named to direct a brand-new school, scheduled to open in Santiago, she would displace no one and inherit no disgruntled personnel. "I seem to be entering the mystic year: 33," she wrote (GM [LG] to MMM, 7 Apr. 1922). She let herself hope.

In her campaign to secure a nomination to Santiago, Gabriela Mistral's strongest supporters were politically active poets from the elite. Poet and architect Pedro Prado presided over urban artisans and intellectuals in the small but strategic "Partido Democrático." Mexican Catholic poet Enrique González Martínez, then serving in his first diplomatic appointment, appealed directly to Chilean President Alessandri. Mistral's alliances with both men reached back in time: Prado had headed a group of madcap modernist artists with whom Mistral had associated, who had called themselves "Los Diez, o el innumerable." As for the Mexican poet-diplomat, she knew how it felt to be an outsider in Santiago. When she had learned that the Mexican poet had yet to receive a single Chilean caller, she lobbied her friends to visit him: "The Mexican poet feels sorely the coldness of his Chilean brethren . . ." (qtd. in Fernández Larraín 161).

In drumming up support for her nomination to Santiago, Gabriela Mistral renewed lapsed communications with former correspondents. Her candidacy's weakness was all too clear. No Radical politicians supported her bid. She made a visit to her strongest political advocate, Pedro Aguirre Cerda, but dared only to request "his neutrality in the struggle" (GM [LG] to PAC, Mar.? 1921). Mistral had reason to worry, as the rival candidate was a woman with university training and a husband, a Mason, with an important position in the Radical Party.

Gabriela Mistral won the battle to secure her nomination. She lost the larger struggle to secure her longer-term future. Trouble came soon. Shortly after the Santiago press reported the news, the rival candidate's supporters published letters that noted the poet's lack of any teaching credential or university degree. Gabriela Mistral was not qualified, they charged. The Ministry of Education was obliged to step in, answering the charge and declining her offer to resign. As she entered the job, she privately resolved to leave after a year, staying just long enough to prove her enemies wrong.

Only after moving to Mexico did Gabriela Mistral describe the antireligious persecution that factored into the next events, leading into the Ministry of Education's withdrawal of support. As in her accounts of childhood trauma, her memory of the insult grew over time. Also like her stories of earlier traumas, her expulsion from Santiago displays the contention between the sacred and the profane, which is an enduring characteristic of *modernismo* (Acereda). Certainly the struggle between sacred and profane formed a core of Mistral's poetry.

In the poet's earliest recollections, she took some of the blame for an unforeseen discussion of religion that destroyed her friendship with "Torreblanca," her school's liaison with the Ministry of Education: "the fanatical spirit was stripped naked in him and in me. . . ." (GM to EB, 5 Apr. 1923). As her health decayed toward her life's end, the poet's account of the long-past battle assumed near-Manichean dimensions. Torreblanca served as but one of many agents within a powerful, secret, anti-clerical Masonic brotherhood that issued "threats of stoning . . . conducted searches of my files of letters, by men who entered when I left." Eventually she cast Torreblanca in that role of the hidden traitor, the Judas who had appeared in her "Motivos of the Passion":

> The ones who got me out were, casually, T[orreblanca] and his wife. I got the nomination and his protection continued. Until one night, when he sat down to copy the draft of "The Teacher's Prayer." Scandalized, astonished, he asked if I really did believe in N.S.J. [Jesus, our Lord]. On hearing my answer, at length, this indelicate man, after listening to my answer to his question, "And what do you see in that?" he answered me. "I see nothing but a man with . . ." —and here an obscenity in relation to the sex of Jesus Christ. Blasphemy always entirely

> agitates me, body and soul. In these words, I told him, "Compadre, you are the sub-secretary of the Ministry and you give the orders throughout this school except in the three rooms where I live. And I ask you to leave now because I have a horror of blasphemy." He arose, trembling, and went out with his wife and children. From then life in Liceo 6 became a misfortune of neglect. I could obtain absolutely nothing for a <u>new</u> school that lacked many things . . . the <u>fence</u> that they had created around me even went as far as Pres[ident] Alessandri. (GM to RT, 1952)

Enduring and recounting attacks was central to Gabriela Mistral's self-fashioning, yet the nationalistically oriented celebration of her figure within Chile minimizes them and silently bypasses her expulsion from Santiago. Rather, her move to Mexico is expressed as an honor for the poet and the Chilean nation. Among Chilean scholars, Jaime Concha uniquely observes the wider picture: "Her life split in almost exactly two halves, and her split is none other than her distance from Chile in 1922: thirty three years at home, thirty four years abroad" (23). Unlike the falsely heroic biographies that present Gabriela Mistral's years of wandering as an affirmation of paternal inheritance and Chilean national character, Concha outlines the bullying that she endured:

> If the girl had been humiliated, if the adolescent hadn't been able to forge a professional destiny, it now befell the young teacher to feel envy and rivalry of her colleagues, big ladies from the comfortable middle class, women with a husband in tow. Worthy representatives of secondary school teaching would make her life impossible in Temuco and would write, years later, in Santiago, anonymous and public letters against her in *El Mercurio*. The accusations? No less than lacking a certified title, a terrible sin that sounds so good in the mouth of mediocre women. (31)

Some writers have suggested that the poet was paranoid (Alone, Rama), but even paranoids can have real enemies. Examination of the poet's archives, now in Chile's National Library, should confirm what scholars have long suggested: Gabriela Mistral received anonymous, poison-pen, "incredibly vile," insulting letters (Scarpa, *Una mujer* 26; Fiol-Matta xxiii; Horan, "Consul" 402).

Ostracized, the poet had scarcely begun working in the new school when she approached her friends from Mexico, asking for their help.

Mexico's Ambassadors of Culture (JULY 1921)

Mexico's Revolution brought many intellectuals into the government to help shape policy. They promoted "Hispanoamericanism," the active development of alliances across Latin American nations as central to Mexico's foreign policy. Cultivating allies from the Spanish-speaking world would insure against the inevitable difficulties with the United States.

José Vasconcelos during his campaign for President of Mexico, 1929

Hispanoamericanism was at its strongest when US–Mexican relations were not faring well. In this case, the worst fighting of the Revolution had passed, but Washington regarded Mexico as overly friendly to Bolsheviks, a rogue state, and susceptible to strong European powers. Oil was the sore point. Mexico held the world's third-largest supply of petroleum reserves, but the 1917 constitution prohibited foreign ownership of land and mineral resources. Mexico lay in ruins after ten years of war. Its government desperately needed to rebuild, but Wall Street stalled on loans, indicating that Mexico would have to honor the lucrative oil contracts established under the deposed dictator, Porfirio Díaz.

Culture promised a way out of Mexico's isolation. The post-Revolutionary Obregón regime offered "asylum and employment to persecuted Latin American intellectuals, the 'pinnacles of the race'" (Blanco 89).[4] The writers who came were politically sophisticated, with the connections and liberal or radical backgrounds enabling them, potentially, to mediate between Mexico and other nations. This wider picture of world diplomacy belies the standard view in which Lucila/Gabriela appears as a Cinderella fairy-tale character, a country girl singled out by hard work and fate, the fortunate recipient of an invitation from José Vasconcelos. Underlying the persistent notion that José Vasconcelos "discovered" Gabriela Mistral is a set of patriarchal assumptions that Grinor Rojo wittily outlines, describing the standard view of the Mistral-Vasconcelos relation: "the Name-of-the-Father, Supreme Phallus, Transcendental Signifier, Master's Voice with and for whom she adopts, conforms, exalts and reproduces the 'Law of the Father'" (Rojo 94).

Contemporaneous documents and evidence of Mistral's longtime connections with Mexican diplomats show that the poet's travel grew out of her networks with numerous leading intellectuals. It was not just that the well-respected poet and diplomat Amado Nervo was an early correspondent. From at least 1919 onward, Mistral was also in contact with Genaro Estrada, who was soon to become a major figure within Mexico's Ministry of Foreign Relations (Zaïtzeff, *Cartas de Gabriela Mistral* 115).

Knowing her skills and the bruising she had experienced, Mexico's ranking diplomat in Chile, Enrique González Martínez, decided to help the teacher. He arranged a meeting when Mexico's most respected educator, Antonio Caso, breezed through Chile amid a lecture tour in August of 1921. Genaro Estrada supported the action from afar.

In Santiago, Gabriela Mistral and Antonio Caso quickly learned that they had much in common. They both regarded teaching as a more heroic than scientific endeavor. Personal heroism had counted heavily in Caso's career. He had stayed in Mexico City throughout the Revolution. Other professors fled for their lives, but Caso remained, "the only professor in the whole University" (Cosío Villegas 49). Foes dismissed his optimism, enthusiasm, and exaltation of the spirit of religion. These very qualities shone forth in Caso's widely attended public lectures on the "psychology of Christianity" delivered in the winter of 1915 at the Díaz de León Theater, then Mexico's largest building. By the light of candles that his disciples brought him when the electricity failed, Caso captivated listeners with his strange face, enormous chin, wild hair, luminous eyes, and forceful, overdramatized speech (Cosío Villegas 56). Chief among Caso's personal heroes was Francis of Assisi, presented as a model of perfect charity: he showed that "the person who performs an act of kindness knows that the supernatural exists" (qtd. in Krause 68-69).

Conferring in Santiago, Antonio Caso and Enrique González Martínez were among the oldest and most conservative of any intellectuals then involved in Mexico's new government. They saw that Mistral had bridged the divide between religious and secularist perspectives. To make the case for inviting her to Mexico, they could point to her regular publications in both Mexico and Argentina. A possible shortcoming: she had shown relatively little attention to social problems in her writing until her recent campaign to be returned to Santiago. At that point, she had written and energetically self-promoted a set of prose poems, "Poemas de las madres," which sympathetically explored the suffering of women who bore children out of wedlock. Crucial to the funding officials back in Mexico was that she had expressed the requisite solidarity with the anti-imperialist message (GM to FHC, 15 July 1921).

José Vasconcelos: "I want an army of educators to substitute for the army of destroyers." (1921)

Engaged in a whirlwind of activity, José Vasconcelos picked up and scanned the telegram from Chile. "I learned," he later wrote, "that Gabriela Mistral, whose fame as a teacher and poet was beginning, wanted to move to Mexico. I immediately followed up with a cable inviting her to collaborate in the Ministry of Education, immediately establishing the date of her arrival in Mexico" (Vasconcelos, *Desastre* 117). That cable, sent in August 1921, coincided with the rapid expansion of Vasconcelos's duties in Mexico and with Mistral's disenchantment regarding her prospects in Chile.

At age forty, Vasconcelos was one of the oldest figures in the upper echelons of a presidential administration that wanted only "those who had recently unpacked" (Krause 102). Ambitious and impulsive, Vasconcelos's energy matched his ambition. An early supporter of Madero, he ran a successful law practice. During the Revolution, he briefly served as director of the federal capital's public schools. In exile, he published books on Eastern religion. On becoming University rector in 1920, he put the state-owned publishing houses under university control. Scandal ensued. " 'What this country needs is to sit down and read the *Iliad*. I am going to distribute a hundred thousand *Homers* in the national schools and in the libraries that we're going to start. . . .' he answered. 'I'll organize the army of educators to substitute for the army of destroyers' " (qtd. in Blanco 104). He sought out artists rather than the middle class, whom he saw as professional sellouts who would jump at the chance to serve tyrants: "I'm looking for young artists who'll capture and draw from popular inspiration, as in past golden ages—Pythagoras, Buddha—when the artist was the servant of the people" (qtd. in Blanco 84).

The constitutional reform that created the Secretaría de Educación Pública (the Ministry of Education, Culture, and Indigenous Affairs) gave Vasconcelos a cabinet-level post from which he federalized Mexico's schools (Fell 49-77). His "army of educators" took over buildings that the Health Ministry had condemned. They printed and distributed 50,000 volumes of classical writers and brought the number of public libraries to 4,500. By 1923 Vasconcelos's offices controlled close to a quarter of the entire federal budget, with a tenth of that devoted to construction (67-76, 106, 193).

José Vasconcelos and Gabriela Mistral coincided in many ways. Both were improvisers who felt comfortable around people much younger than themselves. Vasconcelos extemporized as a writer, politician, philosopher, novelist, and educator, such as when he dwelled on the idea of the mystic or religious educators among the Hindus or past followers of Pythagoras, and when he decided that teachers were to be apostles (Blanco 86). Mistral embodied the idea of the teacher-guru though her physical bearing, which was reminiscent of that of a priestess, and in her poetry's using the language of prayer to inspire and encourage teachers (Blanco 107). Mistral shared and promoted Vasconcelos's ideal of messianic Latin Americanism: "the crisis of teachers is a spiritual crisis: what they tend to lack isn't scientific preparation, but ideals, sensibility and evangelical feeling (excuse the Word)" (GM in *El maestro*, qtd. in García Rey).

Mistral and Vasconcelos also absorbed a huge range of influences: "Buddhism, Zapatism, socialism, constitutionalism, Rodó, Lunacharsky, Carnegie, Romain Rolland, the Greeks, Liberal tradition, Ruskin, trade unionism, Walter Pater, Plato, Pythagoras, Lenin. 'I'm not making history: I intend to create a myth,'" Vasconcelos said (qtd. in Blanco 97). Vasconcelos and Mistral were promotional geniuses in a time and a place when the mass media was developing, almost overnight, on a vast scale. His principles called for conversion: education would make people capable of democracy, converting the masses into citizens. Agrarian reform would convert Indians, who were peons, near-slaves, into landowners. The development of a national culture would reconcile the heterogeneity of the country into a system that followed those of Greece and India, not Rome.

He sent cadres of "maestros ambulantes" and "maestros misioneros" into the countryside to spread education and democracy. "The majority of them had only to change their name to revive, except for spreading the Gospel, the great tradition of Spanish monasticism of the 16th century" (Fell 221).

A chorus of voices has celebrated the "maestros misionarios" program. The dissenting voices merit attention: few of the teachers were prepared for the miserable living conditions in which many indigenous peoples lived (Fell 234). Few had knowledge or experience of the agricultural techniques needed in the countryside; some of the "teachers" were scarcely literate themselves (246). Yet even Vasconcelos's detractors eventually described his offices, the SEP, as "one of the few things that functioned in a democratic manner" in Mexico (qtd. in Blanco 83). In the United States, the press regarded Vasconcelos as looking to sovietize Mexican schools (Blanco 85). The charge was not far wrong. He had devoted part of his exile in San Antonio to reading extensively about the "active educational programs" of Lunacharsky in the Soviet Union (85). Vasconcelos planned something similar in Mexico.

Mistral signed the contract for her appointment to Mexico by January of 1922 but kept the news secret to protect her staff and school. Once the news spread, incredulous journalists pressed her for interviews. As she departed, for example, an interviewer with conservative Catholic newspaper *El Diario Ilustrado* probes lightly, almost insultingly, as if wondering how and why a woman with rough country manners who had attended no normal school or university, a self-taught schoolteacher, had been invited to Mexico. The poet's answer underscored her prestige abroad, where poets had befriended and helped her: "In recent years I've written more often in magazines of Mexico and Argentina than in Chile." She named names: "Amado Nervo, whose patriotic soul shone forth in his precious letters . . . González Martínez, who, when the Liceo was scarcely created . . . hurried to request it for me from President Alessandri" (GM qtd. in Figueroa 95).

Repackaging the rustic poet into an international, even queenly figure required special measures, such as Pedro Prado's lines that compared her to the Virgin Mary, "el último eco de María de Nazareth" (GM, *En batalla*; Horan, "Santa"). Chilean magazines and newspapers, mindful of the advertising revenues from steamships, made her into an icon of modern travel. Ever after she would appear Janus-faced, photographed arriving or leaving. She held no position within Chile's government, yet press reports covered her travel as if it had quasi-diplomatic status, naming the future ambassador-poets who clambered on and off her ship's docks in Peru and Panama. Massive receptions greeted her in Havana. Corresponding to Mexico's anti-imperialism, she saw and criticized the Yankee domination of the northern hemisphere: "Cuba boils with third-rate writers," she reported. "The Yankees run their lives for them. It's quite painful" (GM to EB, 11 Sept. 1922).

Palma Guillén, "as attentive as a tutelary spirit without eyelids"

Awaiting Gabriela Mistral at the Veracruz docks when the *Leerdam* steamed from Havana was one of Mexico's outstanding intellectuals. Palma Guillén, "la Palmita," was short, snub-nosed, dark, cross-eyed, a professor of psychology at the university. Twenty-nine years old, unmarried, from an urban middle-class Catholic family, she was what one of her graduate students later called "a very distinguished, an intelligent woman" who was "really full of herself, because she really deserved to be" (Guadalupe Zúñiga, qtd. in Cano and Radkau 28). Her multiple awards in scientific study made her the seeming opposite of the rustic, homeschooled Gabriela Mistral.

More than forty years after Palma Guillén traveled to meet the poet at the Veracruz docks, the Mexican educator recounted selected aspects of her life with Gabriela Mistral. These focused on the two women's early years in Mexico. Like other writings by Palma Guillén, her reconstructions are at once self-interested and convincing. Brilliant, organized, she was no idle deceiver. Rather, Palma Guillén specialized in suppressing information. She was skilled in disguise and diplomatic retractions. The purpose of her memoir was to protect her long career as a civil servant within Mexico's Partido Revolucionario Institutional (or PRI). Not vanity, but that career led Palma Guillén to shave five years from her year of birth. She was so successful that even her personnel files in Mexico's Ministry of External Relations suppress a key point of evidence: born in 1893, not 1898, Palma Guillén was seventeen years old at the start of the Mexican Revolution. After she had stood in the last class of normal school graduates to accept their diplomas from the hands of the dictator Porfirio Díaz, she had received a scholarship to attend the university, where she led other students in support of Francisco Madero.

Palma Guillén served many masters. She moved from behind the lines of student strikers who sparked the Revolution, to hosting parties for wealthy bankers. A favorite student of Antonio Caso, Palma Guillén was one of the first three students to complete postgraduate studies at the university. Yet Palma did not hesitate to serve Caso's rival, José Vasconcelos, when the latter became the university's rector. Vasconcelos rewarded Palma Guillén quickly and well by giving her a grant to make a year-long tour of Europe with her mother at her side. During that tour Palma Guillén made contacts that she would use throughout her next twenty years of protecting Mexico's interests in western Europe. In the first decade of that work, Palma's "cover" was that she was in Europe to assist Gabriela Mistral.

None of this appears in Palma Guillén's story of how José Vasconcelos summoned her to his new offices at the SEP. Forty-four years later, she recalled his words:

"Palmita, Gabriela Mistral is about to arrive. She's coming to work with us. I would like her to get to know Mexico very well. I want her to see what we have

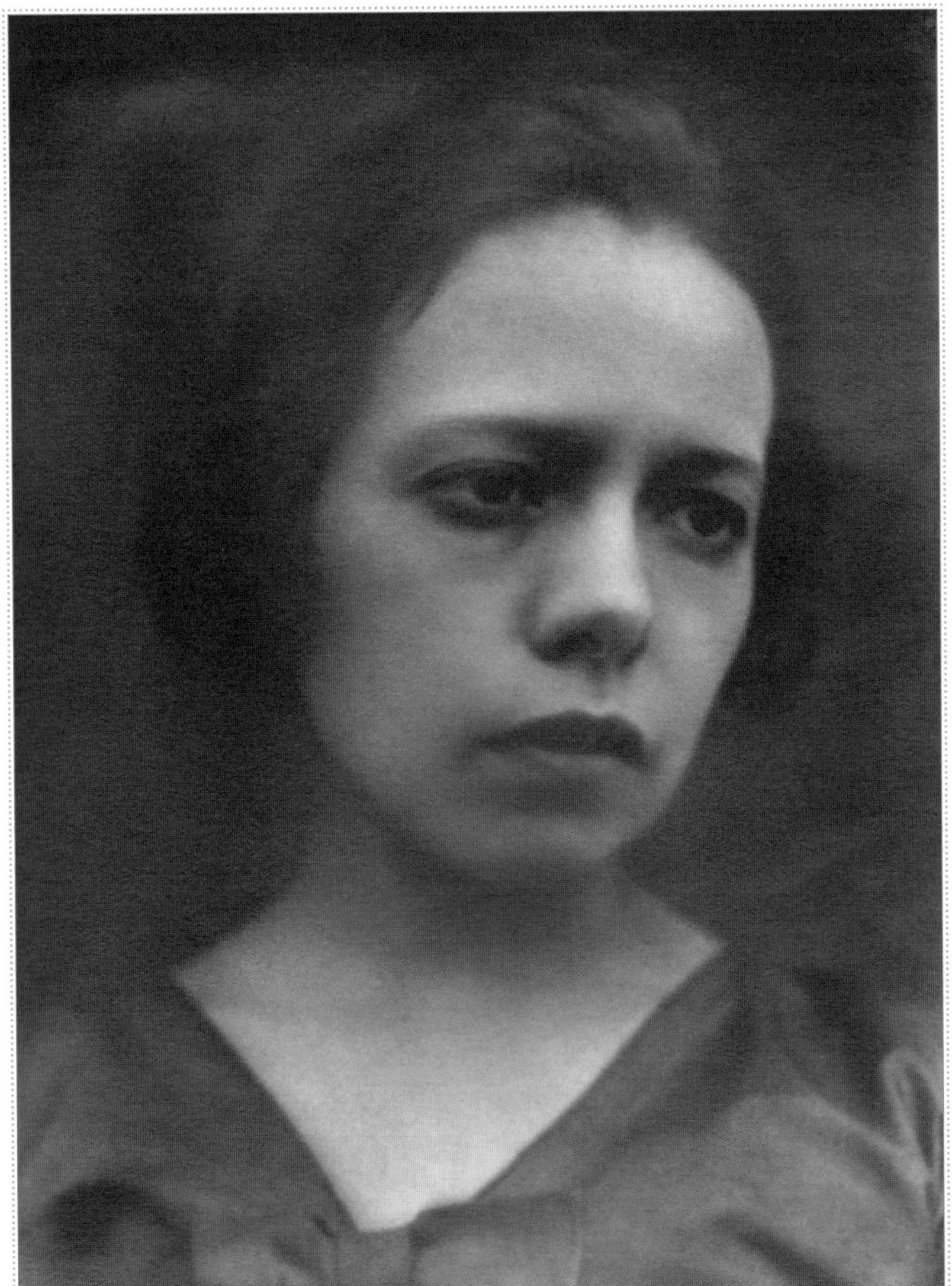

Palma Guillén, about 1918, Mexico

here that's good and that's bad, what we're doing and what we lack. . . . Do you know who Gabriela Mistral is?" (Guillén, "GM en 1922–1924" vii).

"I knew very little," Palma later admitted. "I could honestly say that I knew nothing about Gabriela Mistral . . . some poems in magazines, but nothing of her educational ideas . . ." (vii).

After praising Gabriela Mistral as "genial, an admirable woman," Vasconcelos set forth the challenge:

> I've thought a lot about the person in whom I can confide, to join and guide her. I don't want her to have a partial or erroneous vision of Mexico. I don't want people showing her only what's good or what interests the person who's showing her around. I want Gabriela to see everything . . . travel with her, show her the country: the beautiful and the ugly, the good and the bad, the capital and the provinces—the countryside, above all, the University and rural schools, etc. (vii)

Despite Vasconcelos's reputation for impulsiveness, his staff had weighed the risks. They learned that both women could be hypercritical. An early letter of recommendation recorded Palma as "very intelligent and not without a certain petulant graciousness . . . she could be useful despite her *sense of humor* [English in original]" (qtd. in Torri 269). An ominous warning preceded Gabriela Mistral's arrival from Chile: "and don't forget to wait on Gabriela constantly. She's a woman who needs much close attention" (473).

Old friends routinely develop a standardized story of their first meeting. Palma evoked that story when she described catching her first glimpse of Gabriela at the Veracruz docks. "As I was a conceited girl, she struck me as badly dressed, poorly corseted, with really long skirts, flat shoes and her hair pulled back in a low bun" (Guillén, "GM en 1922–1924" v-vi). The poet echoed those words in recalling how people scorned her as "badly dressed and poorly coifed" (GM to CEE, Sept. 1950). Looking to the contemporaneous record proves more revealing. Gabriela Mistral mentions Palma Guillén in her very first letter from Mexico City, sent as she settled into a luxurious suite at the Hotel Genève. After the poet listed all the attention that she had received, she saved the best for last: "[T]hey've given me a woman who's a university professor for a secretary" (GM to PP, 22 July 1922).

It took some nine months for Gabriela and Palma to firm up their story of "negative first impressions." Ultimately, Gabriela's tribute to her Mexican companion stressed their differences: a letter from 1923 described Palma Guillén as "the only woman that I've known with an effective scientific culture, whom I've wound up admiring, although her braininess initially made her disagreeable to me" (GM to EB, 5 Apr. 1923).

The combination of science and Mexico's decade-long revolution taught Palma an unforgettable lesson: to see the external world, opening her eyes and learning to watch. Everyone who worked alongside Palma remarked on her powers of observation and order. She was, as Gabriela Mistral described her in 1925, "as attentive as a tutelary spirit without eyelids" (GM to CP, 26 Apr. 1925). Small, fine, and quick-talking, an insatiable reader, Palma disguised or suppressed her own voice. Her denials are calculated, seeming to serve others, such as when she denied that she had worked as the poet's secretary (Guillén, "GM en 1922–1924" viii). Her denials point to hidden truths. Although she insisted that she had no interest in writing for publication, she told a friend that two literary genres tempted her: travel and prayer. These were precisely the genres that Palma developed in collaborating with Gabriela Mistral to produce the *Motivos*, that is, the life of St. Francis.

In her life's final days, Palma Guillén admitted to how she worked surreptitiously while living with Gabriela. Whenever she realized that Gabriela was writing poetry, she would watch, feigning ignorance: "I kept quiet, reading, sewing, writing letters as if I didn't realize . . . I watched her like someone who doesn't see, near or far." When the poet had left her notebook, wandering into the garden to read or to water her plants, Palma would rise to remove and copy and carefully return the manuscript, "closing the notebook and leaving it in the same place as if it hadn't been touched," all the while acting with perfect stealth: "Gabriela never surprised me in that chore" (PG to LVS, 28 Feb. 1975).

Often, after the poet had worked over the first version, correcting and crossing out lines and whole stanzas, she would ask, "Palmita, tell me, how does this seem to you?" Then Palma might bring out the original.

"Give it to me, here, how do you have it?" Gabriela would say. "It seems better . . . just let me drop this, or correct that . . ."

"OK," Palma would answer, "but don't go and lose it on me" (ibid.).

Over decades of work as a civil servant, the young woman whom Vasconcelos called into his office became more than careful. She composed herself for photographs that betrayed only a bit of coldness around the eyes. Her tightly pursed lips revealed nothing of the young woman who had remained in Mexico City throughout the Revolution, studying and teaching psychology, ethics, logic, and acting at the university. Amid her rapid rise from serving as Gabriela's secretary to serving as the first woman ambassador from Latin America, Palma Guillén took care not just to organize, but destroy evidence. An orderly typist, Palma systematically hid and destroyed earlier drafts. Faced with inquiries, she denied possessing any manuscripts of value. "I am not among those who believe in retaining the slightest bit of paper written by someone who was a great writer," she insisted (PG to LVS, 15 Apr. 1975). The evidence of her priorities emerges from her organization of the poet's files, in what Palma did not discard: canceled checks, life insurance policies, business correspondence.

Gabriela's arrival in Mexico brought Palma to the task of training and serving her as a queen in a court where physical intimacy marked favoritism and pathways for succession rather than romantic love. Mistral's longtime friend, the Chilean critic "Alone," a quintessential conservative, atheist, and royalist, rightly employs metaphors from court life to describe as "maids of honor" the women who surrounded Gabriela Mistral: "This name [. . .] suits them better," he wrote, "because they're young and beautiful and serve her like a queen" (Alone, qtd. in Spínola 27).

Religion was part of the power that Palma exercised, as the poet later recalled, musing on their first encounters: "I arrived in Mexico and Vasconcelos gave me Palma as a secretary, and she is Catholic, absolutely so, like an Indian woman and like a Frenchwoman in theology, from the family of St. Thomas [Aquinas]. One day she realized and set to the chore of converting me. 'It really bothers me that you wander among Asiatic superstitions'" (GM to GZ, 20 Oct. 1934).

Mexico City's Artists of the Visual: "Cocktail Gabriela Mistral" (JULY-SEPTEMBER 1922)

Four days after Gabriela Mistral's arrival in Mexico, she and Vasconcelos signed new contracts and banquets were held in her honor. That September, the Argentine magazine *Nosotros* reported how the *Revista de Revistas* sponsored one such meal. The menu hewed to the fashion of naming national dishes after writers, in this case, celebrated Latin American women writers:

Cocktail 'Gabriela Mistral'

Crema de Elote a lo 'Juana de Asbaje'	*Juana de Asbaje Creamed Corn*
Arroz con Pollo a lo 'Gertrudis Gómez de Avellaneda'	*Rice and Chicken Avellaneda*
Huachinango Veracruzano a lo 'María Enriqueta'	*María Enriqueta Huachinango*
Barbacoa a lo 'Carmen Lyra'	*Carmen Lyra Barbecue*
Huacamole a lo 'Juana de Ibarbourou'	*Juana de Ibarbourou Guacamole*
Mole de Guajalote a lo 'Alfonsina Storni'	*Alfonsina Storni Turkey Mole*
Frijoles a lo 'Delmira Agustini'	*Delmira Agustini Beans*
Fruta-Café	*Fruit and Coffee*
Cervezas 'Monterrey'	*Monterrey Beer*
Pulques Curados a lo 'Netzahualcoyotl'	*Tequila Netzahualcoyotl*

(qtd. in Galán and Gliemmo 165)

The "cocktail Gabriela Mistral" held equal parts drama and astonishment. Two months of crowds, speeches, and invitations had greeted her arrival. The writer marveled at the metropolis with its million inhabitants. Now she sought seclusion like a lone wolf who had emerged from struggle, disappointment, and public attack. She bought brooms, cups, and saucers and rented a house at the city's edge, in San Ángel, a well-to-do neighborhood of country houses, close to where Vasconcelos had settled his family. There she reflected on her life's transformation, as she related to a friend back in Chile:

> I'll tell you what my strongest impression has been. I came to the house where they've set me up, in the country. I climbed to its roof. The horizon is immense, and I felt the embrace of the light from the sky and the embrace of the silence in all the fields surrounding me. For the first time in eighteen years, I know that I can work in peace, without the sound of the school bell at every hour, without the economic anguish that perennially disturbs my life. I praised God and blessed with all my heart this foreign land that gives me a peace such as this.

"Words with which a future historian of the time could open a chapter on Chilean psychology," her friend answered (qtd. in Alone 37-38).

Urban life did not play a major role in the two women's retrospective stories of their travels in Mexico. Gabriela most often recalled visiting indigenous villagers and peasants and schools that the Revolution had promised to improve via agrarian reform. Palma's account resembles a military campaign, featuring travel by train, truck, horseback, and the hospitality of local partisans. The two women's spotlight on the countryside served the Revolutionary agenda. Hidden, but just as important, was their urban existence: collaborating with others in the Secretaría de Educación Pública, they knew and worked closely with prominent young artists and intellectuals.

Palma and Gabriela each served as models for painters Diego Rivera and Roberto Montenegro, who were among the first artists that Vasconcelos commissioned to decorate the government buildings.[5] Rivera's socialist realism and Montenegro's surrealism lay in the future. As of 1922 and 1923, both painters' work was completely consistent with the Art Deco or Art Nouveau aspects of the *modernismo* that Mistral would develop in writing about the life of St. Francis. Like Gabriela Mistral, the two painters flattered Vasconcelos's Orientalism. They created murals that developed a symbolic style derived from the Byzantine frescos they had seen in Europe. They developed a medievalism that visually translated into the strangely retro modernism that Mistral deployed in the *Motivos* of St. Francis, depicting people, the countryside, geography, botanical life, art, and education.

As the painters chose their models from the people who worked in the buildings they were decorating, Palma Guillén was one of Diego Rivera's models, while Gabriela Mistral sat for Montenegro shortly after Palma had appeared as "Science" in *La creación,* located in the Escuela Nacional Preparatoria. Mistral arrived in Mexico precisely as Rivera was completing this mural, his most overtly religious Christian work. Cast in encaustic and gold, Palma Guillén perches in heaven, a winged, white-robed angel, demure, eyes downcast, although she is presiding over four standing women who represent the cardinal virtues below. Diego Rivera's other model, Lupe Marín, purportedly the most beautiful woman in Mexico, appears opposite and a total of three times throughout. Standing and clothed as Fortitude, she bears a sword; she is also shown seated, listening to music, with three golden apples in her lap. Finally, a kneeling Lupe represents a green-skinned Eve, stupendously naked.[6]

Gabriela watched Palma and Lupe compete for the toad-faced painter's attention. His wild stories, demeanor, even his immense girth captivated people. Diego Rivera scandalized the town, going around with a woman on each arm and declaring himself to be "a male lesbian, a man-eater . . . I'm convinced that humanity marches, in giant steps, toward a bisexual synthesis . . . for that reason I declare myself to be, in the manner of a herald to the advance-guard, a lesbian," he said (qtd. in Espinosa Altamirano 13, 79). His mother reportedly wanted him, her only son, to marry Palma, but Lupe won out (Ribera Marín 136, 168).

Although Palma avoided the mural's unveiling, the newly wed Lupe and Diego pursued her. When they crashed a party held to honor Mistral, the latter turned and rose upon seeing dismay sweep over Palma's face. Mexican writer Elena Poniatowska took Lupe's perspective, reconstructing the rivals' reactions:

> "Let's go, Palmillina," [Gabriela told "la pinacata" Palma Guillén, who was] quite cultured and cross-eyed.
>
> "Huy, a stampede!" Diego chortled. "What the devil does this mustachioed lady with a man's face matter to me, she really does resemble 'America's teacher!' "
>
> Lupe sailed off, Diego trailing. (148)

Determined that Diego Rivera would not upstage him, the painter Roberto Montenegro asked Mistral to sit for a portrait that would appear in the rooms of Vasconcelos's "despacho" (outer office), where people waited for appointments with his assistants. The painter paired the Chilean poet with the noted Argentine "declamadora" (dramatic recitalist) Berta Singerman, another honored visitor of the time. Each stands to one side of the room's main door. Gabriela crouches slightly, looking solemnly outward. Close by, a woman holds in the circle of her arms a swirling orb, the world in her hands. Flanking the scene are Buddhas, Chinese symbols, and a lightly veiled dancing girl. At the mural's far end, a gracious elephant almost dances from the wall.[7]

The portrait made Mistral crow with delight. She called Montenegro "the only representational painter from Mexico whom I both like and admire" (GM to EB, 5 Apr. 1923). Their relationship sprang from their print collaborations and Montenegro's accompanying her in some of her Mexican travels. The contact did not last after Mistral left Mexico. By contrast, Palma Guillén spent time with Diego Rivera when he was between marriages, and proudly owned several of his paintings. Palma's devotion to Rivera amazed Mistral, who cheerfully called him "an utter ogre and Bluebeard even when he doesn't kill the women, but only tosses them aside" (GM to AR and MR, 8 Apr. 1930).

In part from her interactions with the range of writers, artists, and politicians in Mexico at the time, Gabriela Mistral began to develop an appreciation for the value of image and performance (Fiol-Matta 131-55). They all worked the art of the spectacle. Had Pancho Villa not invited Hollywood camera crews to film battles that he and his opponents had obligingly refought when the cameras demanded better light? Reciting poetry and delivering speeches to immense crowds were, like the murals, performances that moved art from the small spaces of the theater and the museum into the open air. The huge scale of Revolutionary Mexico's patronage presented drawbacks that Franco has observed: "[M]onumental art tends to produce icons for simple pedagogy: it reinforces the cult of the artist" (69). Cult or no, these artists of the visual reproduced the double-sided image of Mexico, a new, modern nation that had descended from Aztec courts. The combination required new mythologies of the feminine, with "the mother of the people" and the myth of Gabriela Mistral as "the continent's teacher" replacing the silent and marginal image of the oppressed woman, transforming the myth of "the teacher," joining to it the idea of "redeeming" the Indians, and expanding it to include the women of América (Blanco 110). The student-led backlash against the "New Woman" lay, as yet, a year away (Rubenstein 57-80).

Palace Machinations: Vasconcelos Sent Abroad

(SEPTEMBER-DECEMBER 1922)

Within weeks of Gabriela Mistral's arrival in Mexico, her boss, José Vasconcelos, had to leave town. The trip was not his idea. Rather, President Obregón sent him, as Mexico hoped to develop markets and investments in South America.

Appealing to friends in Argentina and Chile, Mistral hoped that Vasconcelos would be welcomed. Her aid to his cause supported the anti-imperialist ideals then prevailing in Mexico, "where the Latin American union can breathe . . . without the Yankee boot on top of it" (GM [LG] to PAC, 3 Oct. 1922).

Biographer Claude Fell provides details of a trip that began well in Argentina, where Vasconcelos encountered and praised the "real and daily practice of liberty" (606). His weeks there and in Brazil were "serene and triumphal" (620). The results were mixed in Chile, where Eduardo Barrios organized a poorly attended banquet in his honor (GM to EB, 31 Dec. 1922). The Mexican's internationalism met with little enthusiasm after the conservative newspaper *El Diario Ilustrado* reported his declaration that "both Chile and Mexico live a completely feudal regime" (Fell 625). The "insult" of his referring to the army as "the institution which all oppressors have used" also appeared in the Chilean press (628, 632). As Vasconcelos departed, he told a New York newspaper that Chile was "socially divided" (629).

For Gabriela, the visit's nadir involved a botched banquet meeting between Vasconcelos and the Chilean President Arturo Alessandri. The latter had wondered aloud, in front of all present—but addressing Vasconcelos, "Why had Mexico invited Mistral and not her closest rival, Amanda Labarca, as 'the fitting and effective representative of women's education in Chile?'" (GM to EB, 31 Dec. 1922).

Vasconcelos is supposed to have cabled Gabriela in Mexico, reporting his answer: "Convinced more than ever that Chile's best is now in Mexico" (qtd. in Teitelboim 142). But Gabriela Mistral fumed, "I would hear the judgment with perfect calm if these weren't the words of the president speaking to a foreign minister who had brought me and on whom my entire situation in a foreign land depends." She described Alessandri's questions as "hypocritical and malevolent" and "a subtle reproach to Vasconcelos that he didn't know how to choose" (GM to EB, 31 Dec. 1922).

In Mexico, Obregón acted immediately to reap advantages from the insult. The president sent his car to Gabriela Mistral's house in San Ángel. She related the subsequent scene in confidence to Barrios after insisting that he keep it secret. After showering her with attention, President Obregón offered her a commission in Europe working for his government for a year. Her duties would be minimal: "I would write about Mexico and keep my current salary, three thousand Chilean pesos per month, plus my travel costs" (GM to EB, 11 Sept. 1922). While Vasconcelos was abroad, the president continued to seek her out, not only inviting her to his house, but also sending his portrait "with a very affectionate dedication." He sent books to her, the poet related, and proposed to give her a fully furnished library in her home. She was entranced by his generosity, which had, she wrote, "the simplicity of a well-read peasant, because he is very well-read, and has the temperament of an old soldier" (ibid.).

The details of Obregón's proposal emerged bit by bit. He wanted Mistral to stay, working for Mexico for five years, and in exchange for her continued work she would receive an all-expense-paid tour of Europe, accompanied by

Palma Guillén. While Mistral was sorely tempted, Mexico's instability raised questions. "Mexico lives on quivering land. With this enormous social unrest there's no firmness at all in any government" (ibid.). She pointed out that if Vasconcelos left the cabinet, a reactionary would take his place and she would be out of work. To fortify her position, Mistral befriended the diplomats and student leaders that Vasconcelos brought in, such as Victor Raúl Haya de la Torre from Peru. She declined offers to work at the university or address gatherings of diplomats. Rather, by choosing to work in Mexico's populist venues, addressing schools, workers' groups, and teachers' gatherings, Mistral embraced the evangelical rhetoric of public education as a "lay apostle" (Fell 231).

In Michoacán Composing the Life of St. Francis

(CHRISTMAS VACATION, 1922)

Five months into Gabriela's residence in Mexico, Palma decided that she and Gabriela would spend December in the state of Michoacán, where they would visit the cathedral in Pátzcuaro and stay among the fishermen at Lake Chapala. Two of Palma's closest friends who knew the area well assured her that it was both picturesque and, as it turned out, simmering with tensions between the church and the state (Krause 155). Michoacán would supply the largest contingent of "Cristeros," peasants who from 1926 to 1929 engaged in an armed uprising against the state's attempt to suppress the Catholic Church, in which some 90,000 people lost their lives (J. Meyer 9).

Visiting Pátzcuaro, Gabriela and Palma contemplated how Vasco de Quiroga, the sixteenth-century Franciscan jurist, missionary, and contemporary of Thomas More, came to live among the indigenous people in Michoacán. Standing before the massive carved wooden doors of the church that Vasco de Quiroga founded, Mistral grasped several aspects of the man called "Tata Vasco" by the local Tarascan people. His appeal transcended political differences, for he was admired by both "the largely anticlerical intelligentsia of the ruling party and by practicing Catholics, many of whom were opponents of the regime" (Krippner-Martínez 4). Mistral's essay on Vasco de Quiroga, her first concerted effort in writing biography, described him as if he were her contemporary. She portrays him as a teacher of artisans, utopian thinker and urban planner, and a founder of public institutions that offered health care, education, and agricultural work ("Don Vasco," *Lecturas*). He was, in short, a heroic example, not entirely unlike her idealized portraits of Vasconcelos at the time. The writer also finished a short meditation on the charitable works of the seventeenth-century Mexican nun Sor Juana, stressing her humility and charity ("Silueta," *Lecturas*).

Resting by Lake Chapala, as the poet meditated on the generosity she had seen and experienced, she began planning a series of heroic biographies to include the lives of Tolstoy and many others. The profile or sketch would become one of her primary prose forms. As Luis de Arrigoitia's superb study of Mistral's prose observes, her life of St. Francis is one of various essays in which the poet sketches exemplary figures from the past, related to situations in the present (Arrigoitia 61, 197). As opposed to her portraits of living persons, which often grew from interviews, her depiction of Francis of Assisi drew from the surrounding landscape in idealized fashion.

She watched the fishermen working Lake Chapala from the shore. They spread their golden nets, dripping like honeycombs and shining with rainbow-colored fish on the wet sand. Women filed down to the lake, bearing burnished clay pots with which they drew water, hoisting the curved vessels and pressing them to their smooth cheeks. In this rural atmosphere, the poet began praising St. Francis, "el poverello," the little poor man. She wrote as an experienced teacher, presenting concepts one by one. As a poet, she developed the extended metaphors she had learned from *modernismo*, adding the dialogue, parables, and legends that she had learned in producing lyrical description in textbooks to be used in schools. She wrote in gratitude for what living in Mexico after the Revolution had brought to her life. Admiring Michoacán's skillful craft workers and industry, she saw how the Franciscan Vasco de Quiroga had followed the example of Francis as an artisan who would "snatch a bird and sketch out the wings."

The new and lasting admiration for folk arts that came from the poet's immersion in Mexico continued to inspire her: she wrote "La cajita de Olinalá" and "Las jícaras de Uruapan." Each delighted in and promoted the brightly painted, Orient-influenced lacquerware of Michoacán, with its fantastic wild birds, huge insects, and flowers. More broadly, her muse was the "variegated beauty" of the land of Uruapan. As Gabriela Mistral drew close to the end of her first year in Mexico, her letters referred less to her struggles and more to the surrounding landscape: "hills deep with greenery, seas of thick vegetation, black with pure vitality: a generous wine for confronting rich humus for putting on my breast and recollecting it with new vigor" (GM to CP, 1 Apr. 1923). "My eyes are awakened to the earth and natural sciences and by my calm and noble readings." This combination of her readings and the environment made her decide to write heroic biography, focusing on "great lives" (GM qtd. in *Tan* 21).

Time is abolished in her description of Francis's actions, in keeping with other stories about the deeds of saints: "They breach the paper-thin wall between the past and present; seemingly extinct past and unimaginably distant future press into the present" (Brown 81). In his worldly relations, be they with humans, animals, plants, rocks, water or fire, the saint extends a "sense of amnesty, heightened morale" (93). By writing of Francis, Mistral depicts a truth that the philosopher Ortega y Gasset observed: "The virtues which count most for us are those we do not possess." As in her experiences of moving between the city-dwelling elite and the impoverished countryside, she resembles Francis's noble-born brothers in lacking humility. Like his plebian ones, she lacks that degree of refinement or *reverentia*, the high degree of social and cultural grooming that the writer struggles to convey in terms such as "smooth" and "sweet."

After opening with a genealogy that established the subject's Provençal lineage and significant name, Mistral's life of Francis depicts various forms of his communion with the natural world, including his human relations. Throughout all of these, the saint demonstrates the opposite of *rusticitas*, boorishness, slipshodness, and the failure to live a structured life by way of overlooking ceremonious relationships with specific invisible persons. Anyone can behave with *rusticitas* or *reverentia*, depending on context, as appears in the sublime and grotesque story of Francis's encounter with the lepers, toward whom he moves in charity and against the protests of his senses of smell and touch. Possessed by love, he moves from giving alms, mere money, to kissing the outcasts on their decaying mouths from which the lips have rotted away. "You gave and you gave and you gave yourself," Mistral writes (Horan, *Motivos* 50).

Methods and Benefits to Writing About These Heroic Lives

On returning to Mexico City at the year's end, Gabriela told friends that she had completed thirty episodes, "enough for a book," she wrote, that the artist Roberto Montenegro had promised to illustrate. Montenegro apparently completed twelve pictures (GM to EB, 31 Dec. 1922; GM to EB, 5 Apr. 1923). Two of those twelve portraits of Francis, printed alongside the story of Francis curing the leper, were printed in the gorgeous and aptly named *Lecturas clásicas para niños*, to which Mistral heavily contributed.

Aside from looking into the legends of Francis's life, Mistral read closely and carefully Francis's own verses, the *Florecillas*, in a translation by Rivas Cherif. She looked closely at the Franciscan homages of Darío and Nervo, to which she alluded in a new poem, "Mis libros," which resembles Darío's own sentimental literary autobiography in verse. The poem describes her appreciating Francis's *Florecillas* as a respite and relief after the "burning lava" of the Psalms and the vivid screams and fantastic imagery of Dante's *Inferno*. The *Florecillas*, she declares, offers a freshness and "soft plush"

Escuela Hogar Gabriela Mistral, 1923, Zacapoaxtla, Puebla, Mexico

that counters Dante's flames. "I saw that man Francis, as fine as roses / pass through his countryside lighter than a breath / kiss the lily's bloom and the festering breast / in order to kiss the Lord who slumbers within" (Mistral, *Desolación* 1923, 43).

Writing heroic biographies encouraged the poet to move toward the uncertain future of continued work for Mexico and to leave behind the years she had invested in Chile. Rejecting "ferocious nationalism," she looked forward to "calm and noble readings" and "writing great lives" in order "to live my universalism of the spirit, mind, and gaze" (GM qtd. in *Tan de Ud.*, 21). She told her political patron in Chile that while she might eventually travel to Europe "to promote Mexico, at a splendid salary," her immediate future lay in the Americas: "I have been a Hispano-Americanist for years and I don't feel out of place in any country of my language" (GM [LG] to PAC, 1 Jan. 1923).

Transnationalism and writing about heroic lives let the poet reach out to benefactors beyond borders. In the 1923 "autobiography" that she supplied for a chapbook of her poems published in Barcelona, she identified herself as "Christian, completely democratic . . . I believe that Christianity, with profound social sensibility, can save the people." Her allegiance to Mexico and Chile appeared throughout: "I have one school in Mexico and one in Chile. I vacillate between the two. . . ." Her horizon now reached out toward a "larger homeland" that was not a nation but a language, "the language of St. Teresa, Góngora, and Azorín." Nation had no part of the ultimate origins and allegiances that she declared: "I come from peasants and am one of them. My great loves are my faith, the land, and poetry" (GM, "Nota autobiográfica" 5-6).[8]

Writing about "heroic lives" also provided the author with relief from the media's "theatrical or deceitful praise," an alternative to "what is carnival-like in humanity" (GM to EB, 5 Apr. 1923). The instructional or didactic aspect of the heroic life affirmed her sense of worth as a teacher, answering those who had attacked her, and providing "a spiritual boon . . . the soul has lost its coarseness; I feel it to be lighter and infinitely sweeter" (ibid.).

The author's process of creation and revision involved oral composition, a practice that she followed while working in rural villages with Palma Guillén. They set off from the mountains of Puebla, making their way in the sun, dust, and heat before arriving in Jalapa, and then proceeding to the Gulf. In collective story-telling sessions with indigenous peasants, Gabriela and Palma refined these Franciscan texts. The two women developed a repertoire in sites such the rural Zacapoaxtla, "one of the many villages spilled out across the Sierra" (GM to CP, June 1923). They coupled Mistral's stories from St. Francis's life with Dario's and Nervo's Franciscan poems (GM, "Lectura campesina" 97-98). Their storytelling recognized popular devotion, respecting the villagers' taste for religious biography and narrative. Putting the idea of "missionary teachers" into practice, the performances opened as a lecture or actor's monologue begun from far away. She later claimed that her models had been the early Franciscan missionaries, as literacy workers among the indigenous peoples: "As Las Casas and Quiroga and Motolinía learned, what the Indian holds onto, as a secret, loosens up when loyalty is proven. . . ." (97-98).

In an age of tremendous public speeches, large open-air assemblies, and the growth of radio, the speaker aimed for warmth and intimacy, equality between speaker and listeners, teachers and students. Orpheus, whose music made the trees dance, and St. Francis's preaching to the birds were her models: "almost touching them, managing them, annulling all separations of social class, of urban versus rural, between the teacher and the group. Either the group has brought its mentor into itself, or it has arrived on its own and takes charge . . ." (97-98). The best sessions ended, she said, in chorus.

Vasconcelos on Strike, or "putting up with a court, where there's something of everything: philosophers and fools"

(MEXICO CITY, EARLY 1924)

Palma Guillén's and Gabriela Mistral's absence from the capital was not idle tourism. Travel gave them a prudent distance from José Vasconcelos, who had lost many allies with his insistence on linking the university to the government. When the students at the National Preparatory School called a strike in support of the teachers' union, Vasconcelos intervened personally. He strode the five blocks from the SEP to the school's site at the Colegio San Idlefonso. Mayhem resulted. Then he personally expelled the student leaders. When Antonio Caso, then serving as rector of the university, learned of this draconian measure, he resigned in disgust. Vasconcelos's reputation sank still further as he swung between threats to resign and plotting to remain in power after Obregón's term ended. The potential for violence grew, for Mexico had never experienced a peaceful transition. Vasconcelos even made an unsuccessful bid to become governor of the state of Oaxaca, his mother's home state, where he had sent Gabriela Mistral on several visits to address groups of teachers.

Palma's retrospective explanations for why Gabriela left Mexico in April of 1924 make no note of these strikes or rebellions. Rather, the Mexican civil servant asserts that a statue of Mistral, created for the courtyard of the school named for her in the capital, aroused envy amid murmurs about "foreigners" (Guillén, "GM en 1922–1924" x). That anti-foreigner campaign imparted a strong irony to Gabriela Mistral's parting description of Mexico as her "second patria," appearing as "En la otra orilla" shortly before she entered Washington DC on the heels of newly signed agreements between the United States and Mexico. After she had addressed an assembly at the PanAmerican Union, she was quietly debriefed at the Chilean Embassy, where she received a diplomatic passport, her first of many. Unlike "scandalous New York," the US capital seduced and won her over: she did not want to leave "this white and green city, full of fresh air and full of silence" (GM to CP, 25 May 1924).

Back in Mexico, José Vasconcelos was "almost resentful" that Gabriela Mistral had not chosen to travel to Europe with him and his family. He had delayed his departure so that he could preside over ceremonies marking the opening of the gigantic new National Stadium. Gabriela wanted none of it. Writing from the deck of a ship bound for Italy, she offered jocular excuses: "[When] one travels with a king, even with a simple and noble king like that, one has to put up with the court, where there's some of everything: philosophers and fools . . ." (GM to EB, 1 Apr. 1924).

When Gabriela Mistral and Palma Guillén arrived in Naples, they were supposed to be traveling in order to examine and report back on schools. Their actions spoke otherwise, as they set out to interview moderately leftist Catholic and pacifist non-communist intellectuals. A letter that Gabriela Mistral sent to a colleague, a teacher back in Santiago, shows that the poet was presenting herself as "Catholic, but without hatred or narrowness" and engaged in countering communism, "the wave of materialism" covering the world (qtd. Figueroa 178).

Six Months in Europe: Assisi and Spain (MID-TO-LATE 1924)

Whatever the aims of the Mexican politicians who funded this European journey, the poet's mind was often on Franciscanism. As soon as she could, she headed for Assisi, where the Umbrian plain reminded her of the Chilean countryside. She praised the "twelfth-century villages, noble, calm and collected" (GM to EB, 29 July 1924). Here was a refuge: "Assisi is a complete medieval town, but preserved and whose people still have the beauty of very noble architecture amid a mountain plain that is enormously calming. I read and I think calmly. The city is truly Franciscan, tightly gathered like a heart, severe, simple, and silent. I have praised it less than it deserves; it's almost as valuable as the Pobrecillo!" (GM to EB, 16 July 1924).

In Assisi, amid pessimism and melancholy, the poet took the first steps toward becoming a Third-Order, that is, lay Franciscan. "And so I will forever torture myself, in the middle of whatever marvel, such as this Umbrian plain, that is enough for happiness" (GM to EB, 16 July 1924). In unpublished notes, she struggled over her resentment for past suffering in Chile, railing against unnamed literary critics.

Perhaps the two women's relative inexperience in working the gray areas between journalism, public relations, and espionage led to the publication of the poet's anti-fascist remarks. These might have appeared accidentally, for they were published within her report of a conversation with two leading Italian intellectuals. The backlash was fierce: Ada Negri, one of the teachers she had interviewed, repudiated them. The Italian colony in Chile issued a rebuke. But Mistral's published remarks were mild compared to what she wrote about Mussolini's government in a private letter, indicating her revulsion toward "odious fascism, with its uncleanness of armed gangs ruling over the towns, the insolent Black Shirts. . . . Fascism is everywhere, all the time: journalism, literature, industry. Formidable, little brother, voracious, and proud" (GM to EB, 16 July 1924). The negative publicity in Mussolini's Italy contrasted with the two women's more successful visit to Spain, where friends of Mexico squired them about.

Postcard view of Assisi sent by Gabriela Mistral to Eduardo Barrios, 29 July 1924 *(top)*
Excerpt of Gabriela Mistral letter to Eduardo Barrios, 16 July 1924, from Assisi *(bottom)*

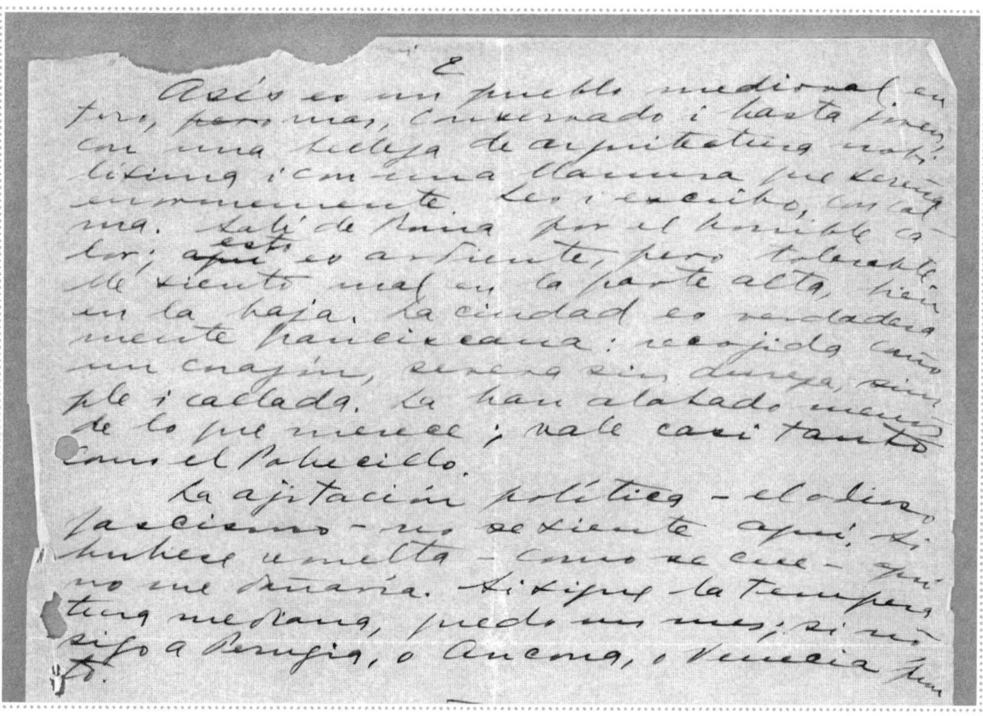

2

Asís es un pueblo medioeval en-
tero, ~~por~~ más, conservado i hasta fines
con una belleza de arquitectura nobi-
lísima i con una llanura que serena
enormemente. Leo i escribo, con cal-
ma. Salí de Roma por el horrible ca-
lor; ~~aquí~~ esto es ardiente, pero tolerable.
Me siento mal en la parte alta, bien
en la baja. La ciudad es verdadera-
mente franciscana: recojida como
un corazón, serena sin dureza, sim-
ple i callada. La han alabado menos
de lo que merece; vale casi tanto
como el Poverello.

La ajitación política — el odioso
fascismo — no se siente aquí; si
hubiese revuelta — como se cree — aquí
no me dañaría. Si sigue la tempera-
tura mediana, quedo un mes; si no,
sigo a Perugia, o Ancona, o Venecia pron-
to.

As Gabriela Mistral prepared to leave Europe, sailing from Spain's Atlantic port at La Coruña, she presented a public reading from the *motivos*. Arranging the reading was the Uruguayan consul; the public was an association of "artesanos" from local factories. The poet opened by noting the Spanish tradition of "respect and veneration toward women" and naming the religious example of St. Teresa along with the noted feminist Concepción Arenal. She moved on to describe St. Francis as "eminently Latin" (qtd. in Molina 313).

In the selections that the poet chose to read, she celebrated the body and the senses. "Everything has lips," she read, naming both "the plowed furrow" of the earth, and "the lips of the sea . . . wide and numerous . . . spilling over with that wild pleasure that makes the seagulls hoot." Francis's lips, by contrast, "seemed small to him for kissing the world, and he began to sing songs." His lips, she concluded, "were made for compassionate song," while he wandered across this world with his feet, "as if it were a borrowed and priceless tapestry" (Horan, *Motivos* 30, 60). She read of how Francis "loved the lark more than any other bird, for its flight straight to the sun," as the human soul's ascent might be, "a winged dart gathered [in] its momentum and singing, suspended between the sun and the world" (Horan, *Motivos* 44).

Aftermath of a Conversion (1925)

Shortly after returning to Chile and formalizing her retirement from the schools, Gabriela Mistral made a public profession of faith, consonant with the Franciscan rule of the time, established under Leo XIII. Conflicting reports greeted her next actions, reflecting the ongoing controversy over the roles of religion and the church in Chile's public life. The poet's earliest biographer, Figueroa, on the side of Chile's Radicals, relates her "conversion to Catholicism" and "alleged entry into the Third Order of St. Francis" as the actions of a decadent poet wracked by psychic pain: "She began to speak quietly and slowly, with a neurasthenic reluctance. Her tiredness is apparent, her exhaustion, her physio-psychological starvation. She explained and convinced. She was the living Word of eloquence" (Figueroa 161). Figueroa then underscores the political power of Chilean schoolteachers: "The teachers who listened, many of them non-believers, almost all of them revolutionaries, burst into applause for the speaker, not for her doctrines, but the form in which she expressed them, as 'the priestess of the word'" (162).

Shortly after Mistral's announcement, the poet María Monvel took a more personal approach, interviewing her in Santiago. "Gabriela Mistral has cloistered herself in a house for workers in Población Huemul . . . choosing a neighborhood like herself: new, clean, simple, and clear. The plaza resembles a village cemetery in spring. The houses have wide windows, light, and absorption" (Monvel 164).

Despite the presence of various people in the poet's small house, working in the background, bringing her materials, organizing her papers, and more, Monvel reported an intimate conversation that ranged over questions such as whether Gabriela Mistral would like to have children (her answer: not at the moment). Hearing the interviewer's observation that the poet's recent writing seems more mystical than before, Mistral clarified. "My mysticism was sentimental. Now I'm Catholic and moreover, I belong to the Third Order of St. Francis." There were no special rules, she said. "I'm free. It's an order for free Catholics. I have, of course, duties. For example, I should give at least ten percent of all I earn, and other things" (qtd. in Monvel 166).

Asked which countries most influenced her Catholicism, she answers, "all of Italy . . . and Spain." The topic of Hell surfaces; the writer indicates that she fears it. Why? "I don't know how to forgive," the poet observed.

"I think you judge yourself wrongly," came the answer, but Gabriela Mistral insisted: "No, that's how it is." It was not that she wished people evil. Rather, she said, "I don't forget. True forgiveness is forgetting" (167).

More intimate still is the poet's description of her life since leaving Assisi, contained in letters to fellow poets such as the Mexican Carlos Pellicer:

> Franciscanism, the third brotherhood, has done me great good and evil. It has loosened from me all the past and the present, without leaving me with anxiety for the future. The Pobrecito [St. Francis] is terrible and makes ashes; not everything in him is roses. I asked for the tremendous release, so much that it came, and it is a mortal spectacle, what the mystic norm achieves inside one, even in the immensely imperfect way that I attain it. (GM to CP, 26 Apr. 1925)

She identified, as ever, with the outsider:

"One suddenly howls like a wolf on the steppes, with solitude and liberty." Her travels to Spain made her hope to return in the future: "I pray to God asking to die in Spain, in a country village" (ibid.).

Although she hoped to finish her "San Francisco" by the year's end, she told the poet Juana de Ibarbourou that her mood was often dark as she struggled to readjust. "I've been a desperate spirit, bitter and 'steeped in the vice of bitterness' like a diabolical drug" (GM to JI, Mar. 1925). Writing to friends in Mexico, she indicated that she hoped Vasconcelos might win the Mexican presidency, but in a far-distant, hypothetical future, when the country's "moral atmosphere . . . becomes as transparent as the light of the meseta" (GM to MGM, Apr. 1925).

Friendship mattered most of all. She told Carlos Pellicer of the love that drew her toward him and to Palma:

> [H]uman beings came to this world only to learn everything and to improve by way of love, friendship, and pity. All else is extra: culture, social life, ingenuity, good taste, a comfortable house, cities. The meaning of friendship, much more difficult than love or charity, becomes more prodigious for me every day, exquisite, perfect. To defend the ones whom one loves, to ameliorate their lives, to communicate to them the news of the soul, so that they can have as much as they can of an inner life, to consolidate each one in another and to give sustenance in turn. The old sense of the family has moved me in this respect: it is only a form of intimate friendship, not something apart. (GM to CP, 14 June 1925)

In Paris with Alfonso Reyes; Cristeros and Sandinistas (1926-1928)

Two years intervened between the last of the Franciscan *motivos* that Mistral wrote in Mexico and her resuming work on the text in 1926. In Chile she announced plans to start a school in La Serena, but her friends in Mexican and Chilean diplomacy knew of a far better use of her talents. They arranged for her to work in Paris at the League of Nations, aided by Palma Guillén. The latter's extra-official presence benefited Mexico, which had been excluded from the League at its founding. In turn, Palma was more than happy to join the poet, traveling from Mexico to Chile and from there to Buenos Aires, where the two women caught a boat to France.

The two women's funds did not go far in the City of Lights. Coming to their rescue was the writer Alfonso Reyes, second in charge at the Mexican Embassy. He was the son of slain General Bernardo Reyes, governor of the Mexican state of Nuevo León under Porfirio Díaz. Alfonso Reyes was one of the most respected writers in Spanish. He had been living abroad for more than a decade, in France and Spain. During Mexico's Revolution, he had moved between employment in diplomatic service and freelance writing in Madrid. Friendship with Mistral would prove a boon to both writers' careers, with Palma Guillén serving in an intermediary role.

Reyes's diary details his pleasure in visits from Mistral and Guillén: "We've held extremely long conversations, for whole days. Palma gets better all the time, and Gabriela is much more intelligent than even José Vasconcelos believes her to be" (*Diario* 1: 123). An experienced diplomat, Reyes knew better than to detail the topics of their conversations. It's clear, however, that he recognized the two women as a team. He compared Gabriela to "a big mountain along whose slopes the thunder rumbles," while Palma, who had earlier catalogued his library in Madrid, struck him as "a marvel . . . more human all the time, and more precise in her thinking" (123). When the two women frequented his home in Paris, they often stayed past midnight. "The night before last I chatted a long time with Palma Guillén and Gabriela Mistral. It's incredible the point to which we were talking. We laughed like babies and we told stories" (176, 184).

Only in France could the three friends speak so freely. The rise of military and other dictatorships made Paris into an epicenter of a transnational, Spanish-speaking "republic of letters." Mistral frankly lamented conditions in Chile, with its "plague of cowboy boots," her code term for a military-sanctioned, one-candidate presidential election that created a new wave of political exiles.

Conditions in Mexico were bleak. The new president, Plutarco Elías Calles, instigated active repression of the Church. He began with strict enforcement of the anticlerical aspects of the 1917 constitution, which limited Church properties and educational activities. New laws imposed heavy fines on clergy who wore vestments. Priests expressing antigovernment sentiments could be sentenced to five years in jail. Calles's motives sprang from personal antipathy—he was a vocal atheist—and politics. Where Obregón had promoted Hispanoamericanism and declared the Revolution to be over, Calles argued that the state and the Revolution were one and the same (J. Meyer 21). His broader goal was to develop the nation-state "through a centralized system of control and repression intolerant of any alternative" (207).

At first, Catholics responded with boycotts of all public events. The Calles regime answered by seizing church property, closing the monasteries, convents, and religious schools, and expelling all foreign priests. Wealthy Catholics relented, but several rural states exploded in a rebellion that united peasants and landowners against federal troops. That rebellion, called the "Cristero War," or "la Cristiada" after the rally cry of the combatants, "¡Viva Cristo Rey!," was especially fierce in rural Jalisco, Zacatecas, Guanajuato, and Aguascalientes (266, 271).[9]

Gabriela Mistral's friends did not denounce the persecution. Reyes's diaries show that he regarded critics of the government, even his own brother, as reactionaries whose possible return to Mexico gave cause for alarm. Wary of becoming targets, the poet's Catholic friends silently headed off to Europe.[10] The wealthier, more conservative ones headed for Spain. The poets headed for France.

Unlike her Mexican friends, Mistral used her correspondence to denounce "the stupid and empty persecution going on in Mexico" (GM to JGM, 8 Dec. 1926). In the quasi-public forum of a personal letter to her friend Joaquín García Monge, the editor of Costa Rica's well-regarded *Repertorio Americano*, she declared that the persecution was "the reverse of medieval fanaticism . . . Catholicism, the religion of 12 million inhabitants, is being persecuted in acts of piracy and violence that aim at tearing a huge Indian and Spanish mass from their faith" (ibid.). She complained of how her allegiances with Mexico prevented her from writing more openly: "I'm too tied to that country and to the Ministry of Education to be capable of setting forth my bare and hostile thoughts about what's been happening with religion" (ibid.). Her first public response to the Cristero revolt was a strangely muted article about education (GM, "La imagen de Cristo en la escuela"). Its philosophically based argument bore the distinct marks of Palma Guillén's thought. Arguing from liberal doctrine, the author indicated that decency required respecting religious institutions of whatever creed.

Decency, as the two women understood it, was in short supply. Vasconcelos's actions were beginning to be an embarrassment. It was not just that he had declared himself to be "a bitter enemy of the government of Mexico" (GM to JGM). In letters to a male friend, Vasconcelos describes dropping his wife and children at the beach on the French Rivera before making off to spend several weeks in Biarritz, drinking champagne at cabarets with one of his mistresses (JV to MG, 2 Feb. 1927).

Signs of Mistral's shifting her allegiance from the scandalous Vasconcelos to the widely respected Reyes had already appeared. She and Palma Guillén had been helping Reyes in his diplomatic career. They repaid his hospitality through the swift and broad publication of several laudatory, polished articles. With Reyes's promotion and transfer to serve as Mexican ambassador in Buenos Aires, the two women found Paris at once less attractive and less affordable.

Heading for Provence was Gabriela's choice. In the village of Bédarrides, near Avignon, the city of the Popes or Anti-Popes, Gabriela stayed "in a rustic mansion surrounded by gardens, whose third floor was full of hundreds of books, in total disorder," continuing her work on the *Motivos of St. Francis* (Carrera Andrade 337). The "mistral" winds pummeled down the Rhône, close by, turning its surface so white that it seemed like a river of almonds. In winter, the house shook with cyclonic force. In the tepid warmth of noon she sat outside, swathed in wool, meditating on the yellow, gray, and ochre sky. While Palma traveled, Gabriela wrote about St. Francis, drawing from her anguish about the Cristero revolt and her pleasure in the Mediterranean summer.

In this last sustained work on the Franciscan *Motivos*, Gabriela Mistral added to her already-drafted materials. She created a book by adding new chapters on the saint's childhood and his encounter with the lepers. She explained the Franciscan community's origins in the friendship between Francis and his first disciple, the noble and rich Bernardo de Quintaval. Perhaps she felt that Mexico was testing her as Bernardo had tested Francis. Throughout the icy Parisian winter of 1926 and into 1927, she had reread Francis's "Canticle of the Sun," which entered into her praises of the elements of water and fire that she wrote at this time. Those very Franciscan and Mediterranean *elogios* and *estampas* also showed the combined influence of multiple writers in Spanish, from the Mexicans Alfonso Reyes and Julio Torri to the Catalan Joan Maragall. She read a biography of Francis by French academician Abel Bonnard as well. Embracing a clarity and simplicity of language and image, the poet abandoned the darker prose of *modernismo*.

That autumn in Provence, the poet offered the volume for publication to a friend who requested it (GM to BC, 1 Sept. 1927). She described the book as "half-finished," but nonetheless proposed that Francis's story appear alongside the closely related *elogios* and *estampas*. Nothing would come of it. Nor did she follow up when the noted French poet and translator Francis de Miomandre praised the *motivos* for their air of childhood and family life. He even begged to translate them free of charge (FM to GM, 27 Oct. 1929 and 10 Feb. 1930).

Standing in the way was the scandal of Vasconcelos's public behavior and the situation in Mexico, which made increasing demands on the two women's time.

Headlong toward Disaster: Mexico (1927–1929)

In the long tradition of exiles, Vasconcelos used his residence in France to plot his political comeback. From the pages of his magazine, *La Antorcha*, he attacked real and perceived enemies. In letters, he began urging friends to return to Mexico, "that murderous and atheistic country" (JV to CP, 22 May 1927). When Guillén and Mistral joined him on the French Riviera, his increasingly erratic, grandiose behavior alarmed them, as Mistral reported to Reyes: "We were with Vasconcelos in Nice and in Bandol—he was with his wife and children. He goes around as if maddened—no exaggeration—by the meeting with the famous Elena [Arizmendi]," one of his former lovers (GM to AR and MR, 16 Sept. 1927).[11] To show contrition, Vasconcelos made a highly publicized visit to Palestine and Greece, followed up with some expressions of resentment that Gabriela and others doubted him: "I never converted," he writes, "because I never stopped believing; I am the worst of all sinners . . . I look at my life, whipped about by evil passions, sensuality and laziness." Vasconcelos persisted in believing that he could practice a love at once sacred and profane: "No men or women in my Father's Kingdom, we will all be like the angels . . . I go forth, ruminating on the philosophy of the Father in addition to the philosophy of the lover that many Christian mystics have taken from pagan ideology" (JV to CP, 7 Apr. 1928).

The hand of Palma Guillén and her friends helped shape the letter, stinging with rebuke, that Gabriela Mistral sent to Vasconcelos. As she wanted to dissuade him from campaigning for the Mexican presidency, it created an enormous distance between them. The letter opened smoothly and followed with the accustomed flattery. "God has given you brains in order to lead. . . ."

Only after she had compared him to the continent's great teachers Sarmiento and Las Casas did the writer begin enumerating his weaknesses, beginning with his susceptibility to flatterers. This undermined his "strength as an intellectual," for his listening to adulation revealed his "fragility as a pseudo-leader . . . a pretender to the heroic, a candidate for national hero." Pushing further, probing the wound, she argued that his utter indiscretion had ruined his chances of attaining political power. "You have made a banal spectacle of your intimate life," she charged. "You traveled, swaggering about like a . . . Mexican Lord Byron, but without having the genuine vocation for sentimental waste. . . ." Although gratitude and friendship kept Mistral from publicizing the break, she was unequivocal that she could not support his efforts to attain any public office. "Retire to your books," she told him, "like Quevedo . . . to salvage what remains of your prestige. Your mother and all of your friends will be thankful for it" (GM to JV, 2 Oct. 1927). The letter reflects Mistral's impatience with the romantic follies of men, especially when they had lofty ambitions. She was more understanding and forgiving of women such as Delia del Carrill, Neruda's wife, whose love for Neruda clouded her mind and judgment as "a woman utterly in love, changed, all turned around by her passion" (Mistral and Ocampo 94). Mistral saw and condemned Vasconcelos for becoming a type of Latin male that she later evoked as "un Nerudita"—excessively concerned with virility, needlessly combative, and oblivious to how his demands created difficulties for those around him (GM to PG, 17 Apr. 1943).

After Palma had helped the poet draft and send her explosive letter to Vasconcelos, the increasing disorder and violence in Mexico demanded Palma's full attention. Obregón had been assassinated in July of 1928, just three weeks after his reelection to the Mexican presidency. The certainty of disorder accelerated Palma's plans to return to Mexico "to help her family," or so Gabriela explained. The truth was harsher: Palma's association with Vasconcelos left her no choice but to return to Mexico and work loyally at the university, where she faced striking students, spies in her classes and in assemblies, and "two big Indians to keep her from getting a thrashing" (GM to AR and MR, 8 Apr. 1929).

Palma Guillén's close, attentive presence had previously enabled Mistral to publish four or more articles a month. With the Mexican's absence the poet's productivity decreased. Gabriela Mistral did manage, however, to produce a somewhat hastily written, strongly worded article in limited circulation. Without Palma's restraining hand, the poet addressed the failed efforts of fiercely secular "Jacobins" to stamp out religion. The consequences, she wrote, were only violence and death, "and no diminution of religious feeling" (GM, "Jacobismo," 1929).

In Mexico, Vasconcelos's presidential campaign rattled toward disaster, concluding with cries of fraud and his calling his followers to take up armed insurrection. After Mistral and others pleaded for his life, Vasconcelos was allowed to leave the country. The machinery of the one-party state ratcheted into place: the US government recognized the opposing candidate put forth by Calles. Breakfast negotiations between Calles and Dwight Morrow, the "ham and eggs" US ambassador, produced concessions to foreign businesses. Despite an agreement with the Vatican, skirmishes between the government and Cristeros continued. Mexico's aid to the Nicaraguan Sandinista rebels, a policy that Mistral had strongly supported, completely stopped. The nation closed its doors in a policy of "México por los mexicanos." Immigrants had to possess a passport, be literate, and demonstrate means. Post-Revolutionary Mexico's collective enterprise and utopianism vanished. Agrarian reform lost intensity.

Most discouraging throughout 1929, the year when Gabriela Mistral had hoped to finish writing her life of St. Francis, was the news from Chile. The poet was in Provence that July when she received the hard news of her mother's death. She told several friends of how she felt cut off, adrift, like a water-plant severed at the root, or with her soul in ashes on the ground. Compounding her sense of helplessness and loss were the effects of the worldwide economic depression. Chile's decision to prohibit the payment of pesos beyond its borders left Gabriela Mistral penniless in Europe. Former friends such as the pious and aristocratic María Luisa Fernández de García-Huidobro, to whom Mistral had earlier dedicated her "Poemas de las madres," now mocked the journalism on which Mistral depended for her entire income: "There's been an article published in *El Mercurio* with Mistral playing up the Countess of Noailles," María Luisa told her son Vicente, the poet. "Have you seen how an anarchist will turn into a noble? . . . What ideas to take root! Better to be an old-fashioned reactionary and live far away from everything that stinks of Denmark" (MFGH to VGH, 1929).

Economic necessity forced the poet's return to the classroom after a decade's absence. A series of visiting professorships in the United States and Puerto Rico, beginning in 1930, gave her enough income to remain in Europe and pay for the care and schooling of her four-year-old nephew, Juan Miguel Godoy. Over the next decade, she and Palma looked after the boy, moving him from school to school as the two women officially entered and climbed the rungs of government service.

Poetry, Diplomacy, and Personal Tragedy in a World at War

When Palma Guillén and Gabriela Mistral were reunited in Spain in 1934, the poet was on her way to completing a volume of poetry, *Tala* (1938), her first in sixteen years. The Argentine Victoria Ocampo agreed to publish this text, its proceeds to be devoted to children exiled and orphaned by the

Spanish Civil War (Mistral and Ocampo 61-66). The volume opens with a dedication "to Palma Guillén, and in her, to the piety of the Mexican woman." It closes with notes on how the poet's spiritual certainties had crumbled following her mother's death, creating "a wide, dark dwelling . . . a country where I lived for five or six years, that I loved for my mother's sake and hated because my soul was in the tumult of a long religious crisis. The so-called 'fruits of pain' are neither good nor beautiful and I wish them on no one" (GM, *Tala* 155). She wandered through a pagan land, conversant with its ghosts:

> I haven't been your St. Francis
> body curved in an arc of "amen,"
> suspended between heaven and earth
> like the crest of dawn
> scaling the lime-tree
> where you once heard the deer and the mourning dove
> This land of many creatures
> has called me and wanted to hold me;
> it touched me inside, like a mother;
> giving itself, a faithful woman.
> It spread me across its flaming breast,
> Its skin rose up on me, like a cobra
> ("Nocturno de la derrota," *Tala*)[12]

The Spanish Civil War and World War II absorbed the two women's lives as they worked to assist refugees and, in Mistral's case, to sway Brazil, Argentina, and Chile away from supporting the Axis. The stress grew unbearable. The poet suffered a complete breakdown following Friday the 13th of August, 1943, when her nephew, recently turned eighteen, lay agonizing on a hospital bed in Brazil after having ingested arsenic. The hospital chaplain, a Franciscan, heard the boy's confession and told the poet that Juan Miguel had been more than brave. "He [the chaplain] told me three times that he never saw an adult, stricken, confess with such clearness and heights of spirit," she reported (GM to Ester de Cáceres, 14 Oct. 1943).

Palma traveled to Brazil to nurse Gabriela following the mental and physical breakdown. The therapy included a routine of private devotion based on reading the Psalms aloud, which the two women used to compose new prayers. "Every afternoon, from when I arrived there, in Petrópolis, I believe in September of 1943, we would pray together for Yinyin," Palma later recalled.

One of their collaborative prayers appears in the present text: it relates Francis to John the Baptist and Peter the Fisherman as figures who know "what's hidden about the creator." Only in prayer and with Palma close could Gabriela begin to acknowledge what she euphemistically termed the boy's "idle pursuits"—drinking and all-night carousing—and his status as a "discouraged child" who had known little continuity or discipline. The prayer names the stigmata as the evidence and reward of faith.

The 1945 Nobel Prize seemed almost anticlimactic. The poet looked up into the gallery and imagined the boy's ghost. She moved to California, where the money from the Nobel Prize enabled her to buy a house in Santa Barbara, California, amid a grove of old pine trees, halfway between the ocean and the hill where seventeenth-century Franciscans from Spain had established a mission that still stands by a rustling grove of eucalyptus looking down into roses. By 1948, Cold War tensions pushed her from California to the relative haven of Mexico, where Palma worked with her to assemble the final volume of poetry that Mistral published in her lifetime: the acerbic, highly condensed *Lagar* (1954).

Mistral returned to overtly Franciscan themes with her 1950 acceptance of the Serra Prize from the Academy of American Franciscan History. As before, she left Mexico for Washington DC, but without Palma at her side. She boarded a petroleum ship in Veracruz. Accompanied by Doris Dana, a young North American who seemed an ideal traveling companion, she headed off to Washington, once again en route to Italy.

The poet's speech to the historians expressed her hope for peace despite the intensified fighting in Korea. "It is necessary that we Christians try, from now on, to approach the Asian soul, to cross that tremendous geographical and moral abyss" (Horan, *Motivos* 114). In explaining the Serra Prize to her employers back in Chile, the poet stressed its peaceful aims as "particularly desirable in this hour of world crisis" (qtd. in *Vuestra* 146).

Crises always found Gabriela Mistral. After Washington, she headed for Italy, where she was to assume a consular appointment. Shortly after she had arrived she felt the shame of being unable to help her longtime friend and colleague, the exiled poet Pablo Neruda, and his companion, Matilde, who appeared at her door:

> He handed me, in silence, his passport, so that I could add stamped pages, for it had been cancelled. [Neruda was in his second year as a political fugitive, and the Chilean government had issued a warrant for his arrest.] I told him that I didn't have even consular stamps or passports. It was true. They hadn't come yet. Neruda is a very quiet, silent man and he did not make a fuss. But I learned from his half-phrases that he went to Rome on his passport errand and returned "as before." (GM to RT et al., Jan. 1951)

Once the prohibition on Neruda was lifted, Mistral was able to renew the visas, not just for Neruda and Matilde, but for a dog they had adopted, a mutt named Nyon, "allowing his owner to take the dog out of Italy to Chile . . .

Pablo could not stop laughing when he heard about Gabriela Mistral's help. 'A visa for a dog! And why not a passport?'" (qtd. in Feinstein 278-279).

"Not even our Palma is capable of forgetting Mexico for a full hour"†

The best scholarship on Mistral and religion underscores the nondogmatic and intuitive in the poet's writings. Taylor and Vargas Saavedra take seriously the poet's interest in Buddha, relating it to her Christianity; Santiago Daydí-Tolson shows Franciscanism as contributing to Mistral's sophisticated ecological imagination, evident in her late-life *Poema de Chile*. Study of the poet's letters and papers in concurrence with Mexican internal and international politics reveals that although Palma Guillén may have worked hard to develop her friend's Catholic sensibility, she actively discouraged Gabriela Mistral from examining or acting on what the poet called her "Catholic conscience."

Loyalty to the Mexican state involved Palma Guillén in an explicit trade-off. Ensuring Gabriela Mistral's promotion of idealized images of Mexico and its friends would give Palma Guillén access to positions of increasing responsibility. Thanks in part to Gabriela, Palma moved from Mexico's educational bureaucracy into diplomacy, work that paid well and used her skills. Rational self-interest led her to fit the story of Gabriela Mistral in Mexico into the already-oversized legend of Vasconcelos. Within that story, she made calculated omissions of the friendships and collaborations between her, Gabriela, and the largely gay, queer, and occasionally closeted writers who have since been grouped as "Los Contemporáneos" (Irwin), including the writers Xavier Villarrutia, Salvador Novo, and Carlos Pellicer.

Accounts of what the two women and their friends achieved on the magazine *El Maestro* have begun to appear (García Rey). More work remains: *Lecturas para mujeres*, the anthology on which Mistral and Guillén collaborated in Mexico, was published with a lesser-known, complementary text to which the two women also contributed. *Lecturas clásicas para niños* is a vast fantasy of *modernismo*, pre-Raphaelitism, and a *novecentista* childhood that belongs in the history of queer contributions to Latin American poetry, corresponding to Mistral's observation that "the most important poetry is Spanish American poetry inspired in childhood" (qtd. in Fell 503). Palma Guillén omitted to mention that freewheeling text in her introduction to *Lecturas para mujeres,* which chronicled the beginnings of her relationship with Gabriela Mistral.

As Palma Guillén retreated from the larger vision of the Americas, away from transnationalism of the early 1920s, she crossed out the names of writers

†GM to AR and MR, 8 Apr. 1929, *Tan* 53.

who questioned and mocked fervent nationalism, such as Xavier Villarrutia and his lover, Salvador Novo, a sexually marked dandy with plucked eyebrows. Novo's posthumously published memoirs circulated in manuscript during his lifetime, so Palma very likely read or heard of satiric scenes such as Novo's description of the apartment that the two men shared: "With enthusiasm, scissors, needle and hammer, I devoted myself to decorating our 'study.' A cute fat-bottomed idol, which we named San Polencho, hung at the head of the couch or 'sacrificial slab' to preside over the scenes. And an extreme nationalism induced me to employ a small earthenware vessel as the most stylish deposit for the Vaseline necessary for the rites" (Novo, qtd. in Irwin 164-65).

Palma Guillén could have been tempted to include Carlos Pellicer in her account. This bold-voiced, consummate actor had been quite close to the two women and to Vasconcelos. When the latter saw the boy's talents in the "maestros misionarios," Pellicer was posted to Venezuela, where the student organizations bestowed on Vasconcelos the title "El Maestro de la Juventud." When Calles came to power, the deeply Catholic Pellicer left for France, where he became one of the two women's most faithful visitors. That friendship did not survive Vasconcelos's 1929 presidential campaign, for Carlos Pellicer had remained loyal to "El Maestro," even going to jail on his behalf.

A name that Palma Guillén did not suppress was that of Jaime Torres Bodet, a chilly poet and ambitious bureaucrat who had been ordered to join in meeting Gabriela at the Veracruz docks. The young man's social and political ambitions—which he called "duty"—were evident from early on. At the Preparatoria, Torres Bodet had affected an absurd schoolboy's outfit: "shorts, socks pulled up the mid-calf, a flashy, hard child's collar, plus an enormous 'bohemian' tie" (Cosío Villegas 40-41). Although Palma Guillén disliked Torres Bodet, whose "economizing" measures within Mexico cost her a job, he was too politically powerful to ignore. Thus his name went into the introduction with scant explanation.

Palma Guillén's nationalist (rather than transnational or Americanist) celebration of post-Revolutionary Mexico ultimately obeyed Vasconcelos's charge, four decades earlier, to show Gabriela "all of Mexico, the good and the bad." Palma Guillén seems even to have brought Gabriela Mistral to meet with the leaders of the opposition: "[C]lassicists and conservatives, in the reactionary newspaper, *Excelsior*, and Gamboa, Peón Contreras, etc. . . . people from the old regime who gave special consideration to foreigners, because it was their opinion that Mexico needs white blood" (GM to EB, 1 Apr. 1924). Rigorous, orderly, precise, Palma was not distracted by the new doctrine of *mestizaje*, or experimental prose, or libidinous young men.

Gabriela Mistral and Juan Miguel "Yin Yin" Godoy in Copenhagen, 1937

Postrimería/Last Days

An enigmatic and contradictory figure in death as in life, Gabriela Mistral has been paraded by politicians, gawked at by tourists, and labeled with a thousand shallow pieties. The ardor for beauty and social reform that spurred her Franciscanism can be scarcely visible in those who would carry on her name. "Today's Crusades," she wrote, involve "el Pobrecito's struggle with pious laziness" (GM to RT et al., Jan. 1951).

Weeks before she died of pancreatic cancer in New York, Gabriela Mistral signed a will that asked the Franciscans of Chile to administer the profits from her literary estate on behalf of the poor children of her childhood village of Montegrande. After death came, she was buried like a queen, following multiple state funerals and wearing the simple black velvet dress in which she had received the Nobel from the hands of the king of Sweden. There was a silk handkerchief at her throat, probably to cover the incision from the feeding tube that kept her alive during her six days' coma in the hospital. Around her waist was the Franciscan cord with the "harmless knot" that ties the saint and his followers to him and one another. A Franciscan robe was draped over her coffin.

Notes

1 When GM referred to the "biographers" of St. Francis, she had likely consulted two sources then available in Spanish: Paul Sabatier, Francis's leading modern biographer, and Johannes Jorgenson. She shares their portrayal of Francis as a politically engaged romantic, but differs in showing Francis as having a poet's or a mystic's closeness to animals and nature: see Vargas Saavedra, "GM por San Francisco." In France she read Abel Bonnard's life of Francis.

2 GM's continuing interest in Barrios's Franciscan novel is manifest in their correspondence, as she related how she had convinced Mexican friends to read *El hermano asno*, which was published in Mexico soon after: GM to EB, 5 Apr. 1923. Mistral's influence and access to publication funds led to the novel's translation into French: Miomandre to GM, 1929-1930.

3 Teitelboim argues that Mistral moved to Punta Arenas to escape an unhappy love relation with Magallanes Moure, but no evidence supports the claim. Scarpa's compilations demonstrate the productivity of the poet's residence in Punta Arenas, presented as her first and definitive experience of exile.

4 Prior to inviting Mistral, Obregón's regime had invited and hosted the writers Restrepo, Morillo, Valle-Inclán, and José Eustacio Rivera. After arriving in Mexico, Mistral helped arrange an invitation for the Peruvian political leader Víctor Raúl Haya de la Torre.

5 On Montenegro and other artists associated with Los Contemporáneos, see <http://www.ciudadaniasx.org/?el-arte-homosexual-en-mexico-a>.

6 On Diego Rivera's *La creación* see <http://www.conservatorianos.com.mx/3villarreal.htm> and <http://www.abcgallery.com/R/rivera/rivera-2.html>.

7 Diego Rivera later mocked both Vasconcelos and, more subtly, Roberto Montenegro by adding a 1928 mural, also in the SEP building, that portrayed Vasconcelos from the rear, mounted on a tiny white elephant.

8 The poet's class status does not quite match her self-portrayal as a peasant, which she developed while living in Mexico. A characterization as provincial middle class would be more apt, since her mother and paternal grandmother could read and write when only ten percent of Chilean women were literate. Also, her grandfathers each owned land, although that wealth vanished in her parents' lifetimes: see Horan, *GM Artist* ch. 1; on the provincial middle class see Valis, *Culture of Cursilería.*

9 By 1927 the US State Department declared Calles to be a Bolshevik for having aided rebels in Nicaragua and passing laws limiting oil exploration to Mexican-owned companies: J. Meyer 26-29.

10 Days before departing for Spain, the Mexican Manuel Gómez Morín, a lawyer who later founded the Catholic-oriented PAN, or Partido Acción Nacional, described the Cristeros as completely lacking direction: MGM to JV, 3 Mar. 1927.

11 In *Ulises Criollo*, Vasconcelos gives a subjective portrayal of Elena Arizmendi, described throughout as "Adriana." See Cano's very engaging biography, *Se llamaba Elena Arizmendi*, for a fuller account.

12 Yo no he sido tu Santo Francisco
con su cuerpo en un arco de "amén",
sostenido entre el cielo y la tierra
cual la cresta del amanecer,
escalera de limo por donde
ciervo y tórtola oíste otra vez.

Esta tierra de muchas criaturas
me ha llamado y me quiso tener;
me tocó cual la madre a su entraña;
me le di, por mujer y por fiel.
¡Me metió sobre el pecho de fuego,
me aventó como cobra su piel!

(Gabriela Mistral, "Nocturno de la derrota," in *Tala*, 1938.)

WORKS CITED

Acereda, Alberto, and Rigoberto Guevara. *Modernism, Rubén Darío, and the Poetics of Despair*. Washington: UP of America, 2004. Print.

Alone. *Gabriela Mistral: Premio Nobel 1945*. Santiago: Nascimento, 1946. Print.

Arrigoitia, Luis de. *Pensamiento y forma en la prosa de Gabriela Mistral*. Río Piedras: UP of Puerto Rico, 1989. Print.

Barca, Pedro Luis. "La prosa de Gabriela Mistral." *Gabriela Mistral en verso y prosa, antología*. Perú: Santillana/Alfaguara/Real Academia, 2010. lxix-c. Print.

Barrios, Eduardo. *El hermano asno, una novela*. Buenos Aires: Agencia General de Librería y Publicaciones, 1923. Print.

Belmas Oliver, Antonio. *Este otro Rubén Darío*. Barcelona: Aedos, 1960. Print.

Blanco, José Joaquín. *Se llamaba Vasconcelos: una evocación crítica*. México: Fondo de Cultura, 1977. Print.

Bolaño, Roberto. *Los detectives salvajes*. Barcelona: Anagrama, 1998. Print.

Brown, Peter Robert Lamont. *The Cult of the Saints: Its Rise and Function in Latin Christianity*. Chicago: U of Chicago P, 1981. Print.

Cano, Gabriela. *Se llamaba Elena Arizmendi*. Barcelona: Tuesquets, 2010. Print.

Cano, Gabriela, and Verena Radkau, eds. *Ganando espacios, historias de vida: Guadalupe Zúñiga, Alura Flores y Josefina Vicens, 1920-1940*. México: U Autónoma Metropolitana, 1989. Print.

Carrera Andrade, Jorge. *Correspondencia con intelectuales de lengua francesa*. Ed. A. Darío Lara and Claude Lara B. Vol. 2. Quito: Abya Yala, 2004. Print.

Chaves Pacheco, José Ricardo. *Andróginos: eros y ocultismo en la literatura romántica*. Mexico: UNAM, 2005. Print.

Concha, Jaime. *Gabriela Mistral*. Madrid: Júcar, 1987. Print.

Cosío Villegas, Daniel. *Memorias*. México: Joaquín Mortiz, 1977. Print.

Darío, Rubén. "The Wolf's Motives." Trans. Carl Selph. Web. 22 June 2011. <http://members.xoom.it/wordreign/carl21.htm>.

Daydí-Tolson, Santiago. *El último viaje de Gabriela Mistral*. Santiago: Aconcagua, 1989. Print.

Espinosa Altamirano, Horacio. *Inconmensurable, inaudito, inverosímil e inusitado Diego Rivera*. México: EDAMEX, 1985. Print.

Feinstein, Adam. *Pablo Neruda, a Passion for Life*. London: Bloomsbury, 2004. Print.

Fell, Claude. *José Vasconcelos: los años del águila, 1920-1925*. México: UNAM, 1989. Print.

Fernández de García-Huidobro, María Luisa. "To Vicente Huidobro, May 1929." Biblioteca Nacional, Chile. Web. 22 June 2011. <bncatalogo.cl/escritor/AE0000408.pdf>.

Fernández Larraín, Sergio, ed. *Cartas de amor de Gabriela Mistral*. Santiago: Andrés Bello, 1978. Print.

Figueroa, Virgilio [Virgilio Talquino]. *La divina Gabriela*. Santiago: "El Esfuerzo," 1933. Print.

Fiol-Matta, Licia. *Gabriela Mistral: A Queer Mother for the Nation*. Minneapolis: U of Minnesota P, 2002. Print.

Francisco de Asís, San. *Florecillas*. Tr. Cipriano Rivas Cherif. Madrid: Apostolado de la Prensa, 1913. Print.

Franco, Jean. *Decline and Fall of the Lettered City: Latin America in the Cold War*. Cambridge: Harvard UP, 2002. Print.

Galán, Ana Silvia, and Graciela Gliemmo. *La otra Alfonsina*. Buenos Aires: Aguilar, 2002. Print.

García-Huidobro Mc A., Cecilia, ed. *Moneda dura: Gabriela Mistral por ella misma*. Santiago: Catalonia, 2005. Print.

García Rey, Rocío. "Gabriela Mistral, latinoamericanista." *Pacarina del Sur: Revista de Pensamiento Crítico Latinoamericano*. Web. 21 June 2011.

Gazarian-Gautier, Marie Lise. *Gabriela Mistral, the Teacher from the Valley of Elqui*. Chicago: Franciscan World Herald P, 1975. Print.

Gómez Morín, Manuel. "To José Vasconcelos 3 Mar. 1927." MS. Archives Manuel Gómez Morín, Mexico City.

Guillén de Nicolau, Palma. "Gabriela Mistral en 1922-1924." Mistral, *Lecturas* v-x.

———. "To Luis Vargas Saavedra 28 Feb. 1975." Vargas Saavedra, *Otro suicida* 14-15.

———. "To Luis Vargas Saavedra 15 April 1975." Vargas Saavedra, *Otro suicida* 17-18.

Guzmán Maturana, Manuel. "To Gabriela Mistral 12 July 1914." *Boletín del Museo Gabriela Mistral en Vicuña* 2, 26, n.d. Print.

Horan, Elizabeth. "Consul Gabriela Mistral in Portugal, 1935-1937: 'Un policía en la esquina y dos o tres espías adentro del hotel.' " Historia 42.2 (2009): 401-34. Print.

———. "Gabriela Mistral's Alternative Identities 1906-1920." *El Ambiente: Queer Sexualities in Latino, Latin American, and Spanish Writing and Culture*. Ed. Susana Chávez Silverman and Librada Hernández. Madison: U of Wisconsin P, 2000. 147-77. Print.

———. *Gabriela Mistral, an Artist and Her People*. Washington: OAS, 1995. Web. 22 June 2011. <http://www.educoea.org/Portal/bdigital/contenido/interamer/interamer_33/ index.aspx?print=true>.

———. Interview with Doris Dana, August 1983. New York, NY.

———, ed. and trans. *Motivos: The Life of St. Francis.* By Gabriela Mistral. Tempe, AZ: Bilingual P, 2013.

———. "Santa Maestra Muerta. Body and Nation in Portraits of Gabriela Mistral." *Taller de Letras* [Pontifícia Universidad Católica de Chile], 25 (1997): 21-43. Print.

Iglesias, Augusto. *Gabriela Mistral y el modernismo literario en Chile: ensayo de crítica subjetiva.* Santiago: Universitaria, 1950. Print.

Iglesias, Augusto. *Gabriela Mistral y el modernismo literario en Chile: ensayo de crítica subjetiva.* Santiago: Universitaria, 1950. Print.

Irwin, Robert McKee. *Mexican Masculinities.* Minneapolis: U of Minnesota P, 2003. Print.

Julia, Julio Jaime. *Gabriela Mistral y Santo Domingo.* Santo Domingo: Centro de Investigación para la Acción Femenina, 1989. Print.

Krause, Enrique. *Caudillos culturales en la Revolución Mexicana.* México: Siglo XXI, 1976, 2000. Print.

Krippner-Martínez, James. "Invoking '*Tata Vasco*': Vasco de Quiroga, 18th-20th Centuries." *Americas* [Washington] 56.3 (Jan. 2000): 1-28. Web. 23 June 2011.

Leal, Luis. "Situación de Amado Nervo." *Revista Iberoamericana* 36.72 (1970), 485-94. Web. 22 June 2011.

Loveluck, Juan. "Cartas de Gabriela Mistral a Amado Nervo." *Revista Iberoamericana* 36.72 (1970), 495-508. Web. 22 June 2011.

Madac, Abel. "Crítica y réplica literaria." 26 Dec. 1905. Mistral, *GM en la Voz* 26.

Magallanes Moure, Manuel. "To Lucila Godoy." 1 Mar. 1915. Mistral, *Manuel* 76-77.

Manzano, Rolando. "Recorrer la vida desde la vereda contraria." *Patrimonio Cultural* [Santiago, Chile] 13 (summer 2008), 10-16. Print.

Meyer, Jean. *The Cristero Rebellion: The Mexican People between Church and State, 1926-1929.* Tr. Richard Southern. Cambridge: Cambridge UP, 1976. Print.

Meyer, Lorenzo. *El cactus y el olivo: las relaciones de México y España en el siglo XX.* México: Océano, 2001. Print.

Miomandre, Francis. "To Gabriela Mistral." 27 Oct. 1929; 10 Feb. 1930. MS. Archivo del Escritor, Biblioteca Nacional, Chile. Print.

Mistral, Gabriela. *Antología mayor. Vol. 3: Cartas.* Pro. Luis Vargas Saavedra. Santiago: Lord Cochrane, 1992. Print.

———. "Autobiografía" [Interview with M. R. Oliver]. 1941. *Mapocho* 43-44 (1988). Print.

———. "Cómo se ha hecho una escuela-granja en México." Dec. 1922. Scarpa, *Magisterio* 163-71.

———. *Desolación. Poemas.* New York: Instituto de las Españas, 1922. Print.

———. *Desolación. Poemas.* Santiago, 1923. 2nd ed. Print.

———. "Don Vasco de Quiroga." Mistral, ed., *Lecturas* 81-82.

———. *En batalla de sencillez: epistolario de Gabriela Mistral a Pedro Prado*. Ed. Luis Vargas Saavedra, M. Ester Martínez Sanz, and Regina Valdés Bowen. Santiago: Dolmen, 1992. Print.

———. "En la otra orilla." May 1924. *Croquis Mexicanos*. Ed. Alfonso Calderón. Santiago: Nascimento, 1979. 133-34. Print.

———. "La enseñanza, una de las más altas poesías." 1917-1918. Scarpa, *Magisterio* 272-76.

———. *Epistolario a Eugenio Labarca*. Santiago: Anales, 1958. Print.

———. *Epistolario de Gabriela Mistral y Eduardo Barrios*. Ed. Luis Vargas Saavedra. Santiago: Centro de Estudios de Literatura Chilena, 1988. Print.

———. *Gabriela Mistral en la Voz de Elqui*. Comp. Betty Jorquera Toro and Pedro Pablo Zegers. Santiago: LOM, 1992. Print.

———. *Gabriela Mistral: páginas en prosa*. Ed. José Pereira Rodríguez. Buenos Aires: Kapelusz, 1962. Print.

———. *Gabriela Mistral: poesía y prosa*. Ed., sel., pro. Jaime Quezada. Caracas: Biblioteca Ayacucho, 1993. Print.

———. *Gabriela Mistral y Joaquín García Monge: una correspondencia inédita*. Ed. Magda Arce with Eugenio García Carrillo. Santiago: Andrés Bello, 1989. Print.

———. "La imagen de Cristo en la escuela." 1927. Scarpa, *Magisterio* 211.

———. [Lucila Godoy y Alcayaga]. "La instruccíon de la mujer." 8 Mar. 1906. Mistral, *GM en La Voz* 43-45.

———. "Jacobismo viejo y cristianismo nuevo." 1929. Mistral, *Recados* 2: 215-23.

———. *Lagar*. Santiago: Editorial del Pacífico, 1954.

———. "Lectura campesina." 1934? Mistral, *Recados,* 2: 91-98.

———, comp. *Lecturas para mujeres*. 1923. Mexico: Porrúa, 1967, 1988. Print.

———. *Manuel en los labios por mucho tiempo: epistolario entre Lucila Godoy Alcayaga y Manuel Magallanes Moure*. Comp. María Ester Martínez Sanz and Luis Vargas Saavedra. Santiago: U Católica, 2005. Print.

———. "Mi experiencia con la Biblia." Mistral, *Prosa religiosa* 39-46.

———. *Motivos de San Francisco*. Ed. César Díaz-Muñoz Cormatches. Santiago: Edit. del Pacífico, 1965. Print.

———. *Motivos de San Francisco*. Ed. Jaime Quezada. Santiago: Andrés Bello, 2005.

———. "Nota autobiográfica." *Las mejores poesías (líricas) de los mejores poetas*. Ed. Manuel de Montolieu. Barcelona: Editorial Cervantes, 1923. Print.

———. "El oficio lateral." 1949. Scarpa, *Magisterio* 43-51.

———. *Prosa religiosa de Gabriela Mistral*. Ed. Luis Vargas Saavedra. Santiago: Andés Bello, 1978. Print.

———. *Recados para hoy y mañana: textos inéditos*. Comp., sel. Luis Vargas Saavedra. 2 vols. Santiago: Sudamericana, 1999. Print.

———. *Selected Prose and Prose Poems*. Ed., sel., pro., trans. Stephen Tapscott. Austin: U of Texas P, 2002. Print.

———. "Silueta de Sor Juana Inés de la Cruz." Mistral, comp., *Lecturas* 67-69.

———. *Tala*. Buenos Aires: Sur, 1938. Print.

———. *Tan de usted: epistolario de Gabriela Mistral con Alfonso Reyes*. Ed. Luis Vargas Saavedra. Santiago: U Católica, 1990. Print.

———. "To Alfonso and Manuela Reyes." 16 Sept. 1927. Mistral, *Tan* 43-46.

———. "To Alfonso and Manuela Reyes." 8 Apr. 1930. Mistral, *Tan* 53-56.

———. "To Alone [Hernán Díaz Arrieta]." 1930? Mistral, *Recados* 1: 19-22.

———. "To Benjamín Carrión." 1 Sept. 1927, Mistral, *Antología* 152-54.

———. "To Carlos Pellicer." 1 Apr. 1923 [sic: 1924]. Zaïtzeff, *Cartas de la Gran Gabriela* 27.

———. "To Carlos Pellicer." June 1923. Zaïtzeff, *Cartas de la Gran Gabriela* 22.

———. "To Carlos Pellicer." 25 May 1924. Zaïtzeff, *Cartas de la Gran Gabriela* 29.

———. "To Carlos Pellicer." 26 Apr. 1925. Zaïtzeff, *Cartas de la Gran Gabriela* 31-33.

———. "To Carlos Pellicer." 14 June 1925. Zaïtzeff, *Cartas de la Gran Gabriela* 35-38.

———. "To Carmela Echenique de E." Sept. 1950. Mistral, *Vuestra* 101.

———. "To E. Barrios." Jan.-Feb. 1919. MS. Special Collections, Hesburgh Library, U of Notre Dame.

———. "To E. Barrios." 11 Sept. 1922. MS. Special Collections, Hesburgh Library, U of Notre Dame.

———. "To E. Barrios." 31 Dec. 1922 [sic: 1992]. Mistral, *Antología* 96.

———. "To E. Barrios." 15 Jan. 1923. Mistral, *Epistolario de GM* 52, and MS, Special Collections, Hesburgh Library, U of Notre Dame.

———. "To E. Barrios." 5 Apr. 1923. Mistral, *Antología* 104-11.

———. "To E. Barrios." 1 Apr. 1924. MS. Special Collections, Hesburgh Library, U of Notre Dame.

———. "To E. Barrios." 16 July 1924. MS. Special Collections, Hesburgh Library, U of Notre Dame.

———. "To E. Barrios." 29 July 1924. MS. Special Collections, Hesburgh Library, U of Notre Dame.

———. "To E. de Caseres et al." 14 Oct. 1943. *El ojo atravesado*. Ed. Veronika Zondek and Silvia Guerra. Santiago: LOM, 2005. Web. 21 June 2011. <http://www.cyberhumanitatis.uchile.cl/index.php/RCH/article/viewArticle/5821/5689>.

———. "To Eugenio Labarca." Mar. 1916. Mistral, *Epistolario a EL* 27.

———. "To Eugenio Labarca." 1916. Mistral, *Epistolario a EL* 31.

———. "To Federico Henríquez Carvajal." 15 July 1921. Julia 290-91.

———. "To Gonzalo Zaldumbide." 20 Oct. 1934. Vargas Saavedra, *Castilla* 72.

———. "To Joaquín García Monge." 8 Dec. 1926. Mistral, *GM y Joaquín García Monge* 96.

———. "To José Vasconcelos." 2 Oct. 1927. Mistral, *Antología* 159-60.

———. "To Juana de Ibarbourou." Mar. 1925. Mistral, *Antología* 129.

———. "To Manuel Gómez Morín." Apr. 1925. Krauze 267.

———. [Lucila Godoy] "To Manuel Magallanes Moure." 7 Apr. 1922. Fernández Larraín 103.

———. "To Maximiliano Salas Marchán." 17 Sept. 1920. MS. Archivo del Escritor, Biblioteca Nacional, Chile.

———. "To Ossandón de la Peña." 12 Oct. 1912. *Boletín del Museo Gabriela Mistral* 2, 16, n.d. Print.

———. "To Palma Guillén." 17 Apr. 1943. MS. Archivo del Escritor, Biblioteca Nacional, Chile.

———. [Lucila Godoy]. "To Pedro Aguirre Cerda." 1920. Mistral, *Antología* 71-72.

———. [Lucila Godoy]. "To Pedro Aguirre Cerda." Mar.? 1921. MS. Archivo del Escritor, Biblioteca Nacional, Chile.

———. "To Pedro Aguirre Cerda." 3 Oct. 1922. Mistral, *Antología* 90-91.

———. "To Pedro Aguirre Cerda." 1 Jan. 1923. Mistral, *Antología* 99-102.

———. "To Pedro Moral." Circa 23 June 1948. MS. Archivo del Escritor, Biblioteca Nacional, Chile.

———. "To Pedro Prado." 22 July 1922. Mistral, *En batalla* 104.

———. "To Radomiro Tomic, Olaya [Errázuriz de] Tomic, and Carmela Echenique." Jan. 1951 [sic: marzo]. Mistral, *Vuestra* 146-49.

———. "To Radomiro Tomic." Feb. 1954. Mistral, *Vuestra* 224-29.

———. "To Radomiro Tomic." Naples, 1952. Mistral, *Vuestra* 175-77.

———. "To Teresa María Llona." After Oct. 1943. Mistral, *Antología* 366-7.

———. *Vuestra Gabriela: Cartas inéditas . . . a los Errázuriz Echenique y Tomic Errázuriz*. Sel., pro., notas Luis Vargas Saavedra. Santiago: Zig-Zag, 1995. Print.

Mistral, Gabriela, and Victoria Ocampo. *Esta América nuestra: correspondencia 1926-1956*. Intro. and notes Elizabeth Horan and Doris Meyer. Buenos Aires: Cuenco de Plata, 2007. Print.

Mistral, Gabriela, et al., eds. *Lecturas clásicas para niños*. Illus. Roberto Montenegro and Gabriel Fernández Ledesma. México: Secretaría de Educación Pública, 1924. 2 vols.

Molina, César Antonio. *La revista "Alfar" y la prensa literaria de su época (1920-1930)*. La Coruña: Ediciones Nos, 1984. Print.

Molloy, Sylvia. "Sentimentalidad y género: notas para una lectura de Nervo." *Literatura mexicana del otro fin del siglo*. Ed. Raquel Olea Franco. México: Colegio de México, 2001. 203-13. Print.

Monvel, María. "Gabriela Mistral, franciscana de la orden tercera." 9 May 1925. García-Huidobro Mc A. 164-68.

Olcott, Jocelyn. *Revolutionary Women in Postrevolutionary Mexico*. Durham: Duke UP, 2005. Print.

Poniatowska, Elena. *Tinísima*. México: Ediciones Era, 1992. Print.

Rama, Ángel. "La oscura formación de un poeta." *Revista Iberoamericana de Literatura* 1.1 (1966): 109-18. Print.

Reyes Ochoa, Alfonso. *Diario, 1911-1930*. Pro. Alicia Reyes y nota de Alfonso Reyes Mota. Vol. 1. Guanajuato: U de Guanajuato, 1969. Print.

Redondo Magallanes, Mireya. *De mis días tristes: Manuel Magallanes Moure*. Santiago: Biblioteca Nacional, Chile, 1999. Print.

Ribera Marín, Guadalupe. *Un río, dos Riveras: Vida de Diego Rivera 1886-1929*. México: Memorias Alianza Editorial Mexicana, 1989. Print.

Rojas, Gonzalo. "Escrito con L." 2004. *Revista Arquimagia*, 21 June 2008. Web. 22 June 2011. <http://arquimagia.blogspot.com/2008/06/escrito-con-l.html>.

Rojo, Grinor. *Dirán que está en la Gloria (Mistral)*. Santiago: Fondo de Cultura, 1997. Print.

Rubenstein, Anne. "The War on Las Pelonas: Modern Women and Their Enemies, Mexico City, 1924." *Sex in Revolution: Gender, Politics, and Power in Modern Mexico*. Ed. Gabriela Cano, Jocelyn Olcott, and Mary Kay Vaughn. Durham: Duke UP, 2005. 57-80. Print.

Scarpa, Roque Esteban. *La desterrada en su patria*. 2 vols. Santiago: Universitaria, 1980. Print.

———, ed. *Magisterio y niño*. Santiago: Andrés Bello, 1979. Print.

———. *Una mujer nada de tonta*. Santiago: Nascimento, 1978. Print.

Spínola, Magdalena. *Gabriela Mistral, huéspeda de honor de su patria*. Guatemala: Tip. Nacional de Guatemala, 1968. Print.

Taylor, Martin. *Sensibilidad religiosa de Gabriela Mistral*. Madrid: Gredos, 1975. Print.

Teitelboim, Volodia. *Gabriela Mistral pública y secreta: truenos y silencios en la vida del primer Nobel latinoamericano*. Santiago: BAT, 1991. Print.

Torri, Julio. *Epistolarios*. Ed. Serge Zaïtzeff. México: UNAM, 1995. Print.

Valis, Noël. *The Culture of Cursilería: Bad Taste, Kitsch and Class in Modern Spain*. Durham: Duke UP, 2002. Print.

———. *Sacred Realism: Religion and the Imagination in Modern Spanish Narrative*. New Haven: Yale UP, 2010. Print.

Vargas Saavedra, Luis. *Castilla tajeada de sed como mi lengua: Gabriela Mistral ante España y España ante Gabriela Mistral 1933 a 1935*. Santiago: U Católica, 2002. Print.

———. "Gabriela Mistral por San Francisco." Unpublished MS of presentation given in Santiago, 2008. Print.

———. "Introducción." Mistral, *Prosa religiosa* 9-33.

———. *El otro suicida de Gabriela Mistral.* Santiago: U Católica, 1985. Print.

Vasconcelos, José. *El desastre: memorias II.* México: Fondo de Cultura Económica, 1984. Print.

———. "To Carlos Pellicer." 22 May 1927. Zaïtzeff, "Cartas de JV" 39.

———. "To Carlos Pellicer." 7 Apr. 1928. Zaïtzeff, "Cartas de JV" 40-41.

———. "To Manuel Gómez Morín." 2 Feb. 1927. Archivo del Centro Cultural Manuel Gómez Morín, México D.F.

———. *Ulises criollo. La vida del autor, escrita por él mismo.* México: Botas, 1935.

Zaïtzeff, Serge. "Cartas de Gabriela Mistral a Genaro Estrada." *Cuadernos Americanos* 37 (1993): 115-31.

———. "Cartas de José Vasconcelos a Gabriela Mistral y Carlos Pellicer." *Revista Casa del Tiempo* [UNAM, México] (2009): 29-44. Print.

———. *Cartas de la Gran Gabriela a Carlos Pellicer.* México: Resistencia, 2004. Print.